Clocking In

Recent Titles in
The Psychology of Everyday Life

CLOCKING IN

The Psychology of Work

Rudy Nydegger

The Psychology of Everyday Life

 **GREENWOOD**™

An Imprint of ABC-CLIO, LLC
Santa Barbara, California • Denver, Colorado

Library of Congress Cataloging-in-Publication Data

Names: Nydegger, Rudy V., 1943– author.
Title: Clocking in : the psychology of work / Rudy Nydegger.
Description: Santa Barbara : Greenwood, [2018] | Series: The psychology of everyday life | Includes bibliographical references and index. | Identifiers: LCCN 2017044294 (print) | LCCN 2017054710 (ebook) | ISBN 9781440850042 (ebook) | ISBN 9781440850035 (hardcopy : alk. paper)
Subjects: LCSH: Work—Psychological aspects. | Work environment. | Work-life balance.
Classification: LCC BF481 (ebook) | LCC BF481 .N93 2018 (print) | DDC 158.7—dc23
LC record available at https://lccn.loc.gov/2017044294

ISBN: 978–1–4408–5003–5 (print)
       978–1–4408–5004–2 (ebook)

22 21 20 19 18   1 2 3 4 5

This book is also available as an eBook.

Greenwood
An Imprint of ABC-CLIO, LLC

ABC-CLIO, LLC
130 Cremona Drive, P.O. Box 1911
Santa Barbara, California 93116-1911
www.abc-clio.com

This book is printed on acid-free paper ∞

Manufactured in the United States of America

I would like to dedicate this book to the most important men in my life: my son, Austin, and my grandsons, Lucas and Sam—you guys make it all worthwhile.

Love,
Dad/Grandpa/Pada

Contents

Series Foreword

Psychology is the science of behavior; it is the field that examines how and why people do, feel, and think the things that they do. However, in a very real way, everyone is a psychologist. Each of us observes and tries to understand the thoughts, feelings, and behaviors of people we are around, as well as trying to understand ourselves. Have you ever thought, "I wonder why she did that?" Or perhaps, "Why did I do that; it makes no sense." If you have, then you are asking psychological questions. Most people enjoy being "students of human behavior" and observing and thinking about people, human nature, and all of the variants of the human condition. The difference between "most people" and psychologists is that the psychologist has spent many years in school studying and learning about people.

In addition to studying and doing research, psychologists also work directly with people in many settings. For example, clinical and counseling psychologists work with people who are dealing with psychological disorders or are having problems in their lives that require professional assistance, but there are many other branches of psychology as well. Sport psychologists work with athletes and teams to improve performance and team functioning. Industrial/organizational psychologists help workers, managers, and organizations function more effectively and efficiently. Military psychologists deal with military personnel and organizations. Forensic psychologists work with police and other law enforcement organizations to help solve crimes and assist law enforcement personnel. In addition to all of the things that psychologists know about people, for any person, understanding psychology can help take advantage of what psychologists have learned to help all people live better and healthier lives and to deal more effectively with others.

The Psychology of Everyday Life is a series of books that will address many different and important psychological issues and areas, the goal being to provide information and examples of how psychology touches all of our lives on a daily basis. The series will also show ways in which psychological knowledge can help us. These books will address psychological concerns with the most up-to-date and relevant knowledge from the field of psychology. Information from the laboratories, classrooms, clinics, hospitals, and other settings will be brought together to help make sense out of some important and often complex ideas. However, these books will be directed toward readers who are not psychologists, but are interested in learning more about the field and what it has to offer. Thus, the language is not technical but is common language addressing "regular" people. There will be times when professional and technical language may be used, but only if thoroughly explained and related to the issues being discussed.

This series of books will focus on specific facets of our daily lives and show how psychology can help us understand and deal with these issues. A wide range of topics will be covered, from eating to exercising to relaxing to interpersonal conflict. Each book will consist of three distinct parts. Part I will answer the "who/what/where/when/why/how" questions related to the topic. These chapters will examine everything from how the subject manifests in our day-to-day lives and how it impacts our psychological well-being to differences across the lifespan and cultures to what famous psychologists have to say on the subject.

Part II in each book will focus on "real-life" examples and will address many of the issues that were introduced in each book in Part I, but will do so with examples and explanations that will make the issues even clearer. It is one thing to have knowledge, but it is an entirely different thing to be able to apply and use that knowledge, and this is what will be covered by the scenarios and interpretative analyses in Part II. When people read Part II they will begin to see many of the ways in which our daily lives are touched by psychology, and the many ways that psychology can be used to support and help people.

Part III in each book will address the controversial issues related to the book's subject. Like any academic and professional discipline, psychology has many areas where there are spirited disagreements among academics, practitioners, and researchers about important issues in the field. It will be very instructive for people to understand these issues and to see the careful and systematic ways that scholars think about and conceptualize various topics, and to see how they debate, discuss, and resolve some of their differences of opinion. For non-psychologists these controversial issues and how they are addressed will lead to a greater understanding of psychological matters, but also a better grasp of how scientists and professionals deal with differences and controversies and how these disagreements are addressed.

Psychology is a broad and diverse field with many different approaches, theories, methods, and ideas, and to capture this field in its breadth and depth would be impossible in a single book. This series of books, however, will serve as an introductory journey through psychology as it relates to the daily lives of ordinary people. I have been teaching, studying, and practicing psychology for many decades and I can hardly wait to read each of the books in this very exciting series, and I welcome readers to take this journey with me.

—Rudy Nydegger, PhD, ABPP

Preface

Work has been a part of life for all of human existence and is a fundamental and vital element of the human condition. Because work is such an important part of most people's lives and has such an impact on the quality of life, health, safety, education, and happiness, it is unfortunate that psychologists have not directed more attention to work and its place in the psychological and emotional aspects of people's lives. The psychology of work is a relatively new approach to understanding work as a part of human psychology. This approach has proven to be very important as a way of understanding some of the differences in the types of work people do and why they end up in the jobs that they have.

Most Americans spend a significant amount of their waking hours at work, and it is true that most people spend more time at work than they do sleeping, relaxing, or spending time with their families and friends; however, there is not much formal research done on how work impacts people's lives. Although we often talk about how much people like their jobs and whether or not they have a career that they enjoy, most people think about their jobs primarily in terms of the functional impact of their job on their lives. Thus, questions like "How much money do I make?" "How many hours do I have to work today?" or "Will I have a job tomorrow?" are likely the kinds of things most people think about when they actually take the time to consider their working life. We do not have to look very far to see that when we look across cultures, racial groups, sexual differences, social class, and other factors, we can find enormous differences in the role of work in people's lives and the impact it has on them—ranging from a positive and healthy impact to situations that are clearly dangerous, unhealthy, unduly stressful, and really unpleasant.

This book will look at some of the aspects of work in people's lives and try to get a better understanding of work as it relates to the human condition. Part I examines Work in Everyday Life and begins with Chapter 1: What: The Many Forms of Work. This chapter looks at the history of work and the different types of work that have been done throughout history and also looks at work in the world today. Chapter 2: Why: The Importance of Work in Our Lives examines the personal and social reasons why people work and how these factors relate to some of the historical changes in the nature of work. Chapter 3: How: The Positive and Negative Effects of Work examines the changing nature of work and jobs in the world today and some of the positive and negative factors associated with work. Chapter 4: Who: Psychologists' Theories about Work explores some of the theories that psychologists have advanced that consider work and how it fits into our understanding of human psychology. Chapter 5: When: Work throughout the Life Cycle looks at work developmentally throughout the life span and also examines work-related barriers and issues at work as well as some of the factors related to the age of workers and the nature of work today. Finally, the last chapter in Part I is Chapter 6: Where: Work around the World. This chapter looks at some of the differences and similarities of work around the world and examines the broader issue of globalization and how it impacts organizations, jobs, and workers.

Part II of this book addresses various scenarios where a specific problem is identified and addresses very real aspects of the types of issues workers have on the job every day. We will look at these scenarios in depth to try to understand them better and then will offer suggestions and options as to how these scenarios could be resolved. Part III examines some of the controversial issues in the psychology of work where psychologists and other researchers and theorists have arrived at different opinions regarding certain specific issues and examines these differences and their implications.

The last part of the book will provide a directory of resources with books, articles, and websites for people who want more information about topics they may wish to address in more depth. There will also be a glossary of important terms and a bibliography of all the sources of information that this book has utilized.

Acknowledgments

I would like to acknowledge everyone who supported and encouraged me in the writing of this book. Particularly, my wife, Karen, my constant partner who is always there when I need her, and whose expert and sensitive advice always helps keeps my books on track and audience focused. Also, my kids and grandkids are always there with love and support when I need it. Finally, my editor, Maxine Taylor, has been terrific. This is not the routine, polite thanks to the editor—I really mean it. She was available for advice and feedback when I needed it and offered some suggestions that I had not thought of that were excellent. Without exaggeration, I can truly say that this book is significantly better for her involvement.

Part I

Work in Everyday Life

1

❖❖

What: The Many Forms of Work

Work is one of those things that usually sound or feel like something negative. For example, it often seems like work is the opposite of "play" and is therefore not something that is fun. Even little sayings like, "All work and no play makes Jack a dull boy," put work in a negative light. However, as much as many complain about work, it is something that most people will have to do, and we probably even know people who seem to really like their work. What is it about work that people like or do not like? Why do people work, anyway? What kinds of things determine what kind of work a person will actually do? These questions imply that there are psychological factors involved in what work is and how it affects us. Since each person is a unique individual, it should not be surprising that understanding what work means to people is very complex, and there will be many differences among people with respect to work.

We know that people have had to work since the beginning of time, but it is obvious that the nature of work has changed over time and which people do different types of work has also changed. For example, in the past, and even in some parts of the world today, children were and are expected to work in sometimes dangerous and difficult jobs. However, in most countries children are supposed to become educated, to be part of their family and community, to learn the basic tasks of life and self-care, and to play and have fun. Thus, in most cultures, work is seen as being the province of the adults, although children are often given chores and other tasks to complete, but they do not usually have a regular job with specific tasks that are part of a work environment like a factory.

In recent years, some scholars and practitioners have begun studying details about work and how it affects people and looking at the role of work in people's lives and how this relates to family and community life. "The Psychology of Work" is a relatively new area in psychology that addresses some of the questions and issues that are involved with the personal and interpersonal aspects of work. Certainly, social scientists like psychologists, sociologists, anthropologists, and even economists have studied work for years. In fact, one area of psychology called Industrial/ Organizational Psychology (it has also gone under different names in the past like Applied Psychology and Industrial Psychology) has studied work behavior for over a century and has examined things like learning and training, motivation, conflict, communication, and many others. There are also some very scientific subspecialties like Human Factors and Engineering Psychology that study some of the specific elements of work, including things like person-machine interface (how people work with machines). However, these important branches of psychology have addressed many of the important aspects of work but have not delved as much into some of the issues raised in the Psychology of Work like:

1. Why do people work?
2. What determines the kind of work a person will do?
3. How does work affect people, families, society, and organizations?

This book will also look at the ways in which a person's job will affect their lives inside and outside of work and will address many of these issues to help people gain a better understanding of work and its place in people's lives.

One of the things that we know makes work important is the amount of time most people spend working. It is true that most Americans spend at least one-third of their lives working every day, week, month, and year. In fact, it is likely that many people spend far more than eight hours a day working, and for a lot of people, more time is spent at work than spending time with their families, sleeping, resting, or having fun. Since so much of people's time is spent in work, it is very clear that a full understanding of human behavior must involve the study of work and its place in the lives of working people and those around them. It is also true that an understanding of the physical, social, economic, personal, and family well-being of human beings must also involve a thorough and in-depth understanding of work as an important part of the human condition.

In one way or another, most people's social and economic circumstances are affected by their work and their work roles. In fact, when we talk about "socioeconomic status," we are talking about the social and economic standing of a person in a particular social group. The job or profession a person has, how much money he or she makes, what kind of education he or she has, where he or she lives and in what kind of house he or she lives, the kind of car he or she drives, the clubs and groups he or she belongs to—all of these things will determine how people are viewed by others in their relevant social groups, the roles and privileges they have, and the quality of life they enjoy. It also becomes very clear that certain groups in a society are treated differently because of their gender, age, race, physical condition, and many other factors, and this is also found in what kinds of jobs people have, the kinds of education they are given access to, and the extent to which they are able to progress in their career paths. Thus, work is one place where discrimination and prejudice are very evident, and since work is such an important part of a person's opportunities and quality of life, if discrimination in the work environment exists (and it certainly does), then it must be that some people are treated unfairly in their jobs and careers because of circumstances in their lives over which they have little or no control; it is also generally true that these factors typically have nothing to do with how effective a person is or might be in his or her job or profession.

Although some people might question this, it is true that the higher a person's salary and the more respected his or her profession or job, the less job stress he or she experiences. This also applies to high-status executives who work under a lot of stress, but they have the salary and benefits to make up for the apparent challenges. The bigger stress is found in people who do not have adequate benefits, including health care and retirement, and must continually worry about the health of their family and their own ability to support themselves after retirement. Today, one of the biggest sources of stress for workers is the lack of job security, and the very real fear that they may not even have a job tomorrow if the company decides to "balance the books" by laying people off for no other reason than saving money in the short term without even thinking about the implications for the long-term performance of the organization or the unnecessary unfairness to the employees—unnecessary because there might be other ways to decrease costs without having to lay people off. I happen to know of one company that was trying to find ways to make their company look better to keep up their stock values, and one executive had the idea of laying off 15 percent of the employees for a few months to make their cash flow appear to be more secure than it truly was—his reward for saving money by laying people off was a very sizable (over a million dollars) bonus. One wonders if the million dollars that they paid the executive (later of course so it did not show up on the books for a while) might have been better spent by not laying off some of the employees.

Suffice it to say, the work, jobs, companies, and professions are very frequently the sources of discrimination and prejudice that affect many people's lives and perpetuate some of the unfairness that we find in our social and economic systems. In the next part of the chapter, we will look at the evolution of human work throughout history and how work and jobs have changed over the millennia, centuries, and years.

A SOCIOCULTURAL HISTORY OF WORK

From archeological evidence, cave drawings, and early recorded history, it is very clear that work has been part of the human experience throughout all time. We know that the early humans "worked" by hunting and gathering food as well as by caring for the young, elders, and ill/injured members of their social group. Thus, work was more about survival than anything else, although it seems likely that one's place in the social status of a group might depend, at least in part, to a person's skills in providing what the group needed, for example, hunting, gathering, or caring for others. As this era of work history progressed, it is very likely that some people began to specialize in certain types of tasks. There would have been those who were the very best hunters, some who would have excelled in finding and gathering food and water, those who were best at caregiving, some who would have shown talent for making tools and weapons, those who were the best fighters (particularly when conflicts would arise with other groups for various reasons), those who gave the best advice, some who might have been healers and/or religious leaders, and those who would have shown an aptitude for leadership. It is also quite possible that one's position and status in the group would depend on the skills that he or she possessed and his or her value to the social group.

The Emergence of Agriculture

One of the most important changes in human history was the development of agriculture. This not only provided for having a more predictable and sustainable source of food but also changed how people lived; not that hunting and gathering would have ended, but now people did not have to rely totally on these less predictable ways of supporting themselves. Probably the main change in society with the emergence of agriculture was the change from the nomadic life where people had to travel to find enough to eat, clothe themselves, and support their group; agriculture meant having a stable place to live and work and that people did not have to move with the change of seasons or with the migration of animals they depended on. By living in one place, many other things could and did change as well. For example, the kinds of housing that people have could become quite different. Homes could now be more solid, safer, weather resistant, warmer or cooler as the weather dictated, and more permanent.

While the styles of people's lives demonstrably changed with the development of agriculture, so did the nature of society. New social roles and structures emerged, new jobs and professions arose, and, in many cultures, men began to own property whereas women were often relegated to caregiving roles and tasks. With these changes, more hierarchical social structures started to evolve. People owning more land and crops became "more important" and influential and would have others who worked for them who were under the control of the more powerful members of society. Although intergroup conflict prehistorically would have been about control of necessary resources like food and game (and sometimes about the possession of women for breeding purposes), after the development of agriculturally based cultures, conflict was now more based on gaining control of land and the people who lived on it, and this is when political systems became more elaborate and the warrior class began to emerge as a way for the people who were of higher status and who controlled the land to keep their position and advantages. Social groups now had a class of people who were rulers and also had a military to protect their position in society and to guard against invasion from other groups. However, after the agricultural evolution and before the Industrial Revolution, work for most people was difficult, unpleasant, dangerous, and unrewarding, and this was particularly true of the masses who did not own land or businesses. Agriculture was the main type of job in which people were engaged, but now there were also people who were in skilled trades like carpentry, blacksmith, and others. There were also professional military people and a limited number of other professionals (e.g., medicine, law, and clergy). In most cultures, the more prestigious professions were limited to people from wealthy and influential families who were more powerful and better educated.

In most parts of the world, there were only a few people in any social group who were allowed to own land, and this was limited by religion, race, gender, ethnicity, and social connections. Rulers and land owners would justify their positions and advantages by invoking religion (e.g., the divine right of kings, pharaohs being gods themselves) or other so-called rights, and they would maintain and support their position by having a military that protected the kingdom as well as controlled the common people in the society. Clearly, these types of social situations (found in almost all parts of the world) resulted in consistent and often violent discrimination and abuse of populations of people and limited opportunities and the types of work available to people by their role and place in society. For example, if a person wanted to be a clergyperson but he was not a male from a prominent family, it was very unlikely that he would have been allowed such a position in most societies. Of course, there are some exceptions to these conditions, but in large part, a person's plight in life was usually determined by his or her social position and family circumstances.

For most people in this preindustrial-era work was still primarily about survival and what people needed to do to provide for their own needs and the needs of their family. With few exceptions (e.g., some skilled trades and businesses), work was rarely about getting rewards or recognition, gaining a sense of satisfaction from their work, or improving their social status and wealth. In most parts of the world, the role of religious organizations started to become more important in society, and these were usually very closely allied with the power and political systems in society. It also meant the emergence of a class of religious leaders who had distinct and important positions in society. At the same time, education was becoming more important, and formal educational institutions like colleges and universities began to emerge and develop. Not surprisingly, access to education was often tightly controlled and was usually reserved for those from prominent and powerful families and who had the financial resources to pay for it. Consequently, most of the professions that depended upon education remained the province of the privileged classes.

The Industrial Revolution

Although agriculture dramatically changed society and work for humanity, the Industrial Revolution was another major influence that significantly changed society and the way people work. Starting at about 1760 and lasting until the mid-1800s, this social and economic evolution changed almost every element of human lives and work. Certainly, agriculture was a major aspect of the work of many people, but as agriculture got better and more efficient, it was taking fewer people to actually provide the crops, and as populations were growing, new opportunities for work were needed. One of the main social and economic changes that arose with the Industrial Revolution was the increasing urbanization of society.

Factories were built in cities, and workers came to live in the cities where they could get jobs. This led to the concentration of capital in the urban centers (e.g., factories, banks) and also to a concentration of the population into smaller geographic areas to make them available to work in the factories.

Prior to the Industrial Revolution, manufacturing was often done in people's homes with hand tools or very simple machines. With the introduction of industrialization, there was a shift to powered, special-purpose machinery with factories and mass production. The iron and textile industries and the development of the steam engine played central roles in the Industrial Revolution, and there were also considerably improved systems of transportation, communication, and banking. Although industrialization provided many more and different types of manufactured goods and an improved standard of living for some, not all of the changes were beneficial for many people—especially workers. Frequently, working conditions were dirty, unhealthy, dangerous, and exploitive, but workers had few options and almost no rights in the workplace; if they wanted to support their families, they had to just keep quiet and do their jobs. It was not uncommon for factory workers to have 12–14-hour workdays for six days per week and one 20-minute break for lunch in the middle of the day. Child labor and exploitation of women, particularly in the garment industry, were common and largely accepted. During the era in which agriculture was the main type of work that was done, people tended to work on the family farm or with religious orders that provided a sense of connectedness within relationships, nature, and structured social situations. With industrialization, workers frequently had jobs that were simple, repetitive, boring, and very minimally related to the final product that was being manufactured. This led to an increasing detachment of people from their work and from the outcome of their work, which was very different from people working on the family farm or in or with religious institutions.

With this new revolution in the world of work, the nature of work changed dramatically with an increased need for skilled workers. Even then, however, workers were largely looked at impersonally as interchangeable parts in a huge machine, and treating employees like "real people," individuals with unique needs and aspirations, was not evident in many if any large factories. With increased need for more highly trained employees with relevant work skills and basic literacy, new expectations were placed on public schools. It was now the role of public schools to get students prepared to enter the workplace and to take on the new roles of the "worker," which was a different role than had ever been seen in the world history of work. With the changing expectations of schools, there also came about changes in society as school became more of a requirement than an option, and ultimately it became a legal responsibility for parents to insure that their children had at least a basic education that would prepare them for the world of work in the new Industrial Age.

With school and work now taking on different positions in society, there were also changes that would substantially alter people's roles and positions. Now education started to become a way in which people could improve their status and wealth. If factories needed better educated workers, and as most children were getting better education, then it was hardly surprising that some of the more gifted students began to find opportunities to improve their station in life as well as their quality of life. From a psychological and developmental perspective, it also became clear that we needed to add another stage to our conception of human development. It used to be that there was infancy, childhood, adulthood, and old age. With the increased emphasis on the importance of education, we now added a new stage: adolescence. However, it was still clear that school-age life was still about meeting the needs of the populace—business and industry had clear expectations about what they expected from students when they entered the workforce, and this had a lot to do with the type of curriculum that students were exposed to. Further, students still had responsibilities to their families and communities as well. For example, most American students think of their summer break as a well-deserved vacation from the rigors of school. However, the reason that we have the summer break was that when farming was still a very common job for most Americans (until well into the 20th century), the summer "vacation" was provided so that students could work on the family farm during the summer to help their families. Clearly, for most students the summer vacation was far more work than school, and most of them could hardly wait to get back to school so they could relax and play with their friends after school and on the weekends.

With increased and improved education, new jobs and professions began to emerge; however, the working life of most office, factory, and farm workers was meager and frequently very abusive, and the gap between the rich and poor was widening and becoming more obvious and unacceptable to many in society. The abuses of the workplace continued to be so flagrant that ultimately labor unions began to emerge, although they encountered opposition and violent protest from some factory owners, and unfortunately many labor union organizers were physically assaulted and sometimes killed in attempts to prevent them from organizing the workers. Fortunately, some of the unionizing attempts actually did take hold and began to positively impact the work environment, making a fairer, safer, and healthier place to work.

Prior to the Industrial Revolution, the agricultural economy primarily defined the work setting—most Americans (and in most other parts of the world as well) worked on farms or in jobs related to farming. During these times, people did not typically "choose" their work or jobs but simply followed their parents into the family farm or business. During this era, a very small minority of people might actually choose their work and usually for spiritual or personal reasons or because of special talents like art or music. These exceptions were usually for a "calling," which was a skilled trade, profession, or religious work.

With the increasing concentration of capital resources and population in the urban centers, we began to see other changes in society; for example, in the city there needed to be some way to get food from the farms to the people who needed to feed their families, and farmer's markets and trading posts emerged with even more specific needs for workers' skills and knowledge, and this led to the growth of an increasingly important mercantile class where new business people would start making an impact on society and on the economic system. Even in the hunter-gather era, it became clear that specialized work groups could lead to more efficient work, and although this was also true during the agricultural period, it became even more obvious as the Industrial Revolution progressed. There was increasing need for people who were educated, trained, and interested in a specialized and select type of work. This was the time when people started thinking differently about jobs—they now started to focus on "careers." The birth of the career era dramatically altered the ways that people thought about work; it was no longer just about the job but how a person would organize his or her life around a specific career that would define him or her as a person and would establish a life path that would secure a way of life and a future for himself or herself and his or her family. The emergence of careers is one of the major changes in the world of work following on the heels of the Industrial Revolution and flourishing in the increasing opportunities and options in education and higher education as well.

Another interesting development during the Industrial Revolution was the introduction of new theories and ideas about economic systems that would significantly affect work and how work is done and rewarded. For example, approaches like capitalism, socialism, and communism were discussed and debated by scholars, philosophers, workers, and business people. Capitalism is an economic and political system in which a country's trade and industry are controlled by private owners for profit, rather than by the state. Many countries today use some version of capitalism as the basis of their economic system. Socialism is a political and economic theory where the means of production, distribution, and exchange of goods and materials should be owned or regulated by the community as a whole. Thus, the government should own certain things like the police and military, regulatory agencies, highway construction and maintenance, and so forth, but they should monitor and supervise privately owned businesses as well. Communism is a political theory advocating class war leading to a society in which all property is publicly owned and each person works and is paid according to his or her abilities and needs. Some countries have tried to realize communism, but there are no examples of major countries that are totally communistic.

What is very interesting about these economic/political/social theories is that even though they address the issues of workers and society as a whole, they were all developed by wealthy aristocrats with little or no input from the majority of workers who would be affected by these different systems. So although they are theories that address the lives and interests of workers and families, they were developed by people who did not come from the working class at all.

Changing Work and the Development of Labor Unions

As the working conditions and the treatment of workers worsened during the Industrial Revolution, some people started thinking about workers' rights and their ability to stand together and have some strength to confront employers and demand better treatment and safer conditions. Although there are other attempts historically for workers to band together for the betterment of their circumstances, these were uniformly unsuccessful, and the birth of modern labor unions (called "trade unions" by some) can be traced to the mid-19th century in Britain. Pathetic wages, extremely poor working environments, unsafe and frankly dangerous practices, and little attempt made to remedy these situations led to the efforts of some workers to try to band together and hope that a show of strength would get the employers to pay attention to them. Unfortunately, what these attempts usually produced was further abuse, assaults on union organizers, and even cases of murder. In fact, many employers hired "professional union busters" to use violence and intimidation to discourage union organizers. Some companies hired organizations like the Pinkerton Detective Agency, which gained prominence protecting President Abraham Lincoln during the Civil War, and this agency infiltrated unions, threatened and abused union organizers, and would often prevent organizers from going into companies to gain recruits. Because of these kinds of practices, many countries (including the United States) passed laws making it illegal to try to prevent or actively discourage unionization.

The union movement was very successful in improving wages and benefits, restricting working hours, and providing safer and healthier work environments. In the United States, however, over the years, the union movement became less popular, and since working conditions had largely improved, fewer workers felt the need to have union protection, and they felt that unions were no longer needed. Interestingly, in the era of layoffs, lower wages, reduced or nonexistent benefits, and very poor job security, it will be interesting to see if there will be a resurgence of interest in organized labor. However, one of the problems in some unions is a history of abuse and racketeering that linked unions with organized crime, and this led many people to very rightly question what the unions were doing and why they were doing it. It is also true that many unions were not very good at adapting their message and methods to the late 20th- and early 21st-century work environments, and often their messages sounded very much like the union rhetoric of the 1930s.

In the United States today, only about 12 percent of workers belong to a labor union. This number is less than Canada and Mexico in North America, is lower than almost all of the countries in Europe, and is lower than most of the countries in South America. Some might say that workers are treated better in the United States and therefore do not need unions as much. However, one study by an independent consulting group analyzed the working conditions around the world and grouped countries from the best (Level 1) to the worst (Level 5) from the standpoint of workers' rights. Level 1 included countries like Belgium, Denmark, Netherlands, Norway, and Lithuania. The United States was put in Level 4 with countries like Iran, Iraq, Haiti, and Honduras. If labor unions are going to have an impact on the American workforce today, they will need to look at their message and their methods and try to adapt them to the current work environment and address some of the important needs of the modern workers. It would seem that if unions, companies, workers, and consumers could work together more effectively, better results could be had by all. Unfortunately, too often these different groups are seen as having conflicting interests and are often at odds with one another, but there is no reason why this set of circumstances could not be changed for the better.

Work during and between the World Wars

When many of the major powers in the world went to war in the early years of the 20th century, it dramatically changed the workplace for most people—particularly those in the industrialized nations that were involved with the war effort. Before World War I, America was starting to become more urbanized and was transitioning from a largely agricultural country to one focused on manufacturing. Most workplace jobs were held by men, with women largely working as homemakers or in occupations concentrated in lower paying service-sector positions—traditional "women's jobs." Women could be nurses, teachers, secretaries, domestic workers, and retail clerks, but it was unusual to find women in factory jobs other than in the garment industry. Interestingly, with the American entry into World War I, our heavily manufacturing-based economy was challenged to fill jobs vacated by men who joined the service to "fight for their country." The most obvious and available source for new workers was women, and this proved to be a very important contribution to the war effort. Many women joined the workforce and went to the factories and other traditionally "male" jobs to provide the kind of workers necessary to maintain the war effort from the supply side. Of course, these women did not trade being a homemaker for being a factory worker—they now had two jobs and were expected to do both, which most did without question or complaint. In fact, those women who were unable to leave home to work frequently contributed to the war effort by knitting socks for the soldiers, rolling bandages, assembling first-aid kits, and doing other helpful tasks that they could fulfill at home.

Of course, there were men who stayed home to work during World War I for a variety of different reasons. Some were not suited for military service because they were too old or too young, were physically infirm, or were in a protected profession (some farmers, doctors, scientists, merchant seamen, and others whose civilian jobs were essential for the war effort). These men often stayed in their usual jobs, although with a reduced workforce, they often had to do far more than they had before the war. Many men also contributed by becoming volunteer fire fighters or civil defense workers. Clearly, the work environment was dramatically changed during World War I with "soldier/seaman/marine" being the most common job held by men during the war.

After the end of World War I when the troops returned home, women typically returned to their primary job of being a homemaker or working in one of the usual jobs for women at that time. Very few women remained in the factories, and in fact those who wanted to continue working were seen as being unfair to the soldiers who had risked their lives for the country to come home and not find a job because the jobs were now held by women. Consequently, the work environment started to slowly return to the prewar norms with many men working in factories and most women working at home. Between the end of World War I in 1918 and the stock market crash in 1929, the nature of work remained fairly consistent with what had been the norm before the war. However, when the stock market crashed, the work environment changed dramatically, and the changes were largely negative.

The amount of unemployment and the length of the Great Depression were completely unknown in modern America. At one point, over 25 percent of the workforce was unemployed, and many were significantly underemployed and making far less money than what was needed to support themselves and their families. African American men were hit the hardest, and women in all racial groups were able to find jobs more easily than many men; the workplace was far different than in the past. To complicate things further, drought and unwise farming practices in the Plains states led to the "Dust Bowl," and many farms failed and thousands of farm families simply left their farms and headed west for the promise of a new life in California.

Interestingly, one of the industries that flourished during the Depression was entertainment—particularly movies, radio, and music. On a daily basis, people's lives were so miserable that they valued any opportunity to escape into a world of fantasy, fun, and excitement. A night out to listen to live music and dance was also the type of entertainment that people would save their pennies to allow them to get out even occasionally for some respite and break from the tedium and misery that defined most of their lives on a daily basis. Consequently, those involved with the entertainment industry, including actors and actresses, musicians, dancers, and others, were given opportunities to work when many others could not work at all.

When elected, Franklin Delano Roosevelt (FDR) promised to put America back to work and keep us out of any further world wars. By revamping the banking system and putting other financial controls in place to guard against financial depression, FDR started making some headway in financial recovery. He also started the Tennessee Valley Authority (TVA) and the Works Progress Administration (WPA), which gave many Americans full-time and important jobs, building and repairing the roads, dams, and bridges in the country, and many new and important projects were completed while also putting thousands of workers back on the job.

Unfortunately, the one thing that did most to end the Depression was the entry of the United States into the war in Europe. From 1929 to 1939, America was in very dire straits economically, and life during that decade was very difficult for most Americans except for the very rich whose lives did not change much at all. Although many Americans opposed the United States getting involved in another European war, and particularly after the horrors of World War I—"the war to end all wars"—circumstances involving our allies like Britain and France as well as what had happened to Poland, Czechoslovakia, and Austria and many other countries made it increasingly obvious that the United States had to get involved, and we did. Although most Americans cared little about the possibility of war in the Pacific, it was the bombing raid by Japan on Pearl Harbor in Hawaii that led the United States to declare war on Germany and its allies, Italy and Japan.

As in World War I, after the declaration of war, many Americans volunteered for military service and many more were drafted. With an amazingly ambitious mobilization effort, the United States started modifying its impressive manufacturing capabilities to start manufacturing weapons, ships, planes, tanks, trucks, and other types of needed supplies and equipment. This was a huge stimulant to the economy, and suddenly there was virtually no unemployment. Those who could serve, served, and those who could not were left to pick up the slack at home and fill all of the needed and vacated jobs. Once again, women were called on to step up and take on new roles. They fulfilled all of the traditional roles for women in our society, and they also took factory jobs and other traditionally male jobs like driving trucks and taxis. Some women joined the new female branches of the service (WAVES and WACS), and many worked in medical and clerical roles in the military and at home.

During World War II, the country benefited from what we learned in World War I, and it did not take as long to get mobilized and to get the war effort on track as it had earlier in the century. Of course, some men were also left behind because of age or infirmity or because they were in "protected" jobs that were necessary for the war effort. Men and women also worked in law enforcement, fire safety, and civil defense—all roles very helpful to the war effort. It is no exaggeration to say that the support of women and men who fulfilled important roles at home during the war was instrumental in helping the war come to an end as soon as it did. Americans' capacity for hard work and dedication was undoubtedly one of the factors that led to the Allies ultimately winning World War II and also putting the United States into the forefront as an economic and military power to be taken seriously.

Following World War II, America started finding its way back into "normal" patterns of work. Men returned to their jobs and started working again; however, this time women were not so quick to return to "business as usual," and many of them started feeling that they should have the right for education and career options just like their male counterparts. Of course, even though things were changing, the change was gradual and not without its rough spots. For example, this was also the time when African Americans and other people of color started standing up for the rights that they felt they deserved as much as their white male colleagues. The GI Bill was making college education available to more people than ever before and also provided mortgages for former military personnel to make the dream of home ownership a possibility for people who never expected to actually have their own piece of the American Dream.

Working life and life in general was much different and much more pleasant than during the Depression and was certainly better than war. However, largely because of the research that was done during the war and also during the Cold War with the Soviet Union after World War II, new technologies were coming about that would change the world forever. Computers, transistors, microcircuitry, television, rocketry, jet propulsion, atomic power, robotics, and numerous other exciting new prospects were opening up new jobs, new careers, and new ideas not even thought of a few years before. As work in the United States and around the world started to change, we began to enter the Digital/Information Age, and many have referred to this as the "information revolution."

The Digital and Information Age

In the past few decades since World War II, the nature and type of work has changed dramatically. The relationship between workers and their employers has likewise changed, and for many people the idea of job security is completely foreign to their work experience. Today, in many parts of the world, many jobs have been turned over to computers or robots, and often we do not have any contact with a "real person" when we are doing business. Many lower-level service jobs have been replaced by machines, and most of these types of jobs could have been performed by people. Thus, many of these types of jobs are now obsolete for human beings, and these types of jobs might have been the only hope for upward mobility in the job market for many people who do not have the skills or education to enter the workforce in any other capacity.

It is clear that digital technology is replacing skilled, unskilled, and service workers across the entire globe, and it is estimated that about 75 percent of the labor market in most of the industrialized countries in the world perform jobs that require repetitive tasks that do not require much in the way of problem solving or training. If these simple jobs are what most workers are doing, and many of these jobs are being replaced by machines, then this does not bode well for the future of the work environment for most employees or potential employees. Another interesting problem is that digital technology has made it possible for much work to be spread around the world where every employee might be located and then he or she can work remotely through computers and/or telephones. How many times have people called a helpline for a product or service only to be answered by someone who is clearly foreign and is difficult to understand? Since education has become much more rigorous around the world, it is now possible to find educated and trained employees in many places around the world who are willing and able to work remotely. The decision as to whom to hire then becomes a purely financial one—who can I hire that will be the least costly to the company? This may not be the best decision in many instances, but since the "bottom line" seems to rule most business decisions, it is this type of solution that will often be the result. It is clear that in many organizations, there is an increased need for highly trained workers, but since there are trained and educated workers all over the world, companies are very likely to hire the least expensive employees and manage/supervise them remotely. It is also true that many of the jobs that are available are entry-level service jobs, and when employees get more effective and expect increased responsibility and improved salary, the company will just fire them and hire someone who is cheaper to pay. Similarly, many companies are finding that with more of their work being shifted to machines or workers in different parts of the world, there is less need for middle managers, and many companies are finding that they can reduce costs by laying off middle-level managers and just spreading more of the work around with the existing managers and also using digital technology to monitor the work of many employees, making it less important to have as many managers.

Other Changes in the Workplace Today

Globalization

This is a current trend that will continue to increase and affects every business around the world from the biggest to the smallest. By using the Internet, even small business can locate new markets, find new employees, find suppliers to provide the goods and services they need, and explore new opportunities. Globalization is here to stay, and in many ways it has improved the way people shop and do business. It seems obvious that the economic base of our entire society is being rearranged by globalization. Economically, globalization has led to a pervasive spread of free market capitalism. Even in formerly communist countries, it is now very common to see new establishments arise and to see many people opening their own small but very real new businesses. Because of these kinds of changes in global markets and workforces, economic competitiveness has taken over as the prevailing culture, and loyalty today is primarily for the bottom line. Many employers complain that employees are not as loyal as they used to be, but it is also true that employees will only be as loyal to the company as they perceive the company is loyal to them—if the company balances the books by laying off employees, why would the workers feel loyal to the company? The answer is—they will not. Loyalty between company and employee is not largely a thing of the past in most companies.

In this new global environment, education is even more important to get a job, but education and experience do not necessarily lead to long-term careers in the person's area of training. As employees get more expensive, many companies simply let them go and hire someone else at a lower salary. Further, the integration of globalization and technology has resulted in a labor market that is not affected by national boundaries or even by languages. Work and jobs have become more frenetic and harried, and people are working harder and longer as well as having more pressures and needs at home—life for many people today is increasingly stressful, nonrewarding, and difficult. It is hardly surprising that many people resent their jobs, dislike the company their work for, and feel increasingly helpless and hopeless about their career prospects.

The Changing Contract

In the past, employees may have had an employment contract that defined the legal connection between the employee and the employer. In addition, however, there was also a "psychological contract" that defined the informal expectations regarding the relationship between the employee and the employer. This psychological contract usually implied expectations regarding a long-term relationship between the worker and the company, but in today's world, there is very little in the psychological contract that has anything to do with long-term expectations. Now it is likely that the psychological contract is more skill- and responsibility-based and is basically an agreement that if the employee works hard and does not cause trouble, the company with give him or her a paycheck and maybe even some benefits. However, many companies are focused on short-term gains, profitability, and remaining flexible. Therefore, companies are using more part-time, contractual, and other contingent employees to minimize their long-term connections and responsibilities and to keep expenses as low as possible. For example, companies will find ways to hire people who do not have more permanent connections with the organization so that they do not have to pay as much in the way of benefits like health insurance and pensions. Unfortunately, many of the stores people shop in on a daily basis have the very questionable policy of only scheduling employees in a way that keeps them just below the number of hours that would make them full-time—by keeping the employees part-time, the company avoids having to pay them benefits, thus further reducing the sense of connection between the employee and the company.

Changes in Caregiver Work

In most cultures, women provide most of the caregiver work in the home and professionally. However, there is no reason why men cannot fulfill these roles as well, and in recent years, we have seen more stay-at-home dads, more male nurses, and more men working as nursing assistants and home health aides. It is obvious that in many cultures, there are significant changes in the roles in families, and although these changes appear to be reasonable and appropriate in most contexts, it is still not clear how these differences will affect families and society in the future.

Changes in Labor Unions

In 1954, 39 percent of American workers belonged to labor unions, but in the United States today, it is closer to 12 percent, and this is probably due to several factors. Earlier we discussed the facts that unions had some difficulties because of the history of some unions and their association with organized crime. Of course this was not true of most unions but did involve a few of the very visible and important unions, and this altered the way many people looked at unions. We also mentioned that many unions had not adapted very well to changing times and new needs. Some of the specific changes that have affected union membership include changing demographics and unions not focusing on the needs of the new members but trying to maintain some of the past gains they had achieved; also, factors like globalization and politics have impacted the perception and needs for unions. Finally, with so many companies trying to maintain profitability by keeping wages and benefits low, they are not focusing as much on workers' rights and needs but clearly send the message that unionization is not desirable with the implied threat suggesting that supporting unions could result in a person losing his or her job. With job security being a major issue for many employees, taking a position contrary to the desires of management is often perceived as being a very dangerous position to take, and thus there is less likelihood that workers will try to join unions. Many younger employees today see unions as largely ineffective and out of touch and see no good reason to spend money on dues to even join one.

The Working Poor

This has become a very large and important problem in this country and in other areas of the world. We have millions of people in the United States who are working full-time but who have minimal or no real benefits. The very tragic reality for many people is that they have a full-time (or almost full-time) job but have no health insurance, and because they are working, they do not qualify for health insurance programs like Medicaid. For many people with families, they cannot afford to work because they cannot afford to buy health insurance and cannot get Medicaid while they are working. Consequently, there are many people who have jobs but do not have insurance or any kind of pension program. We are going to find in several decades that there are many people who are not in good health because they could not afford insurance or health care, and as they get older, their medical needs will increase and cost even more. Further, these people will be financially unprepared for retirement and will "have to work until they die." Unfortunately, many of these people will end up in nursing homes or extended care facilities, and their cost will be borne by the society as a whole—these are huge problems that are presently not being dealt with effectively.

Summary of Changes for Work in the New Millennium

The new work environment will need new types of workers with different types of skills, abilities, and characteristics. Many work organizations will change from highly regimented and structured to smaller groups that will often work in local settings producing specialized products. Of course, many of these smaller organizations will be owned or controlled by larger corporations, which need what they produce. Because these smaller organizations need to be adaptable to changes in marketplace and in the larger organizations that they depend on, the employees will have to master many different and changing tasks as well. Consequently, workers will need to be socially and mentally flexible and able and willing to deal with frequent and often unanticipated changes, which will require them to master new tasks and demands. Workers who can adapt to these requirements will be most valued. The cognitive attributes that will be needed in the new work environment include excellent technology skills, exceptional problem-solving skills, and the ability to work well in teams and to communicate effectively with other employees. However, it is still likely that most employees will move from one company to another as they are replaced with newer and less expensive and younger employees. With fewer management positions available, people will continue to move from one organization to another to try to improve their position. Although companies will need and value highly trained, flexible, and multiskilled workers, it is still true that most of the available jobs will be for entry-level service-sector jobs, which means that we can expect that a large number of employees in the future will be underemployed since they will be preparing for jobs that may not be as available as they have been led to believe.

WHAT KINDS OF JOBS DO AMERICANS HAVE?

According to the Bureau of Labor Statistics, in 2012, 16.6 percent of American workers had jobs in federal, state, and local governments, and this includes postal workers, military, police, and public education employees. In 2012, 15.3 percent workers were in wholesale and retail trade, which includes things like clothing stores, grocery stores, auto dealers, and so forth; 15.2 percent worked in private education services, health care, day care, and so forth; professional and business services accounted for 13.4 percent of workers, and these jobs included legal services, accounting, administrative services, and IT professions. About 10.2 percent of workers were in the leisure and hospitality industries, including hotels and restaurants, the arts, museums, gambling establishments, and so forth. Only 9 percent of workers were in the manufacturing sector, and some of the smaller job areas were financial activities (5.8%), construction (4.2%), other services (4%), transportation and utilities (3.4%), media and telecommunications (2%), and mining and logging (0.6%).

Compared to statistics in 1972, the jobs in which people "make stuff" for others (like manufacturing) are a much lower percentage today than in the past, whereas jobs where people "do stuff" for others (service-sector jobs) are significantly higher today, and many of the service-sector jobs are in health care, partly because of the increasing age of the population and the increase in medical needs and services. Interestingly, most of the increases in health care involve increased costs for drugs, services, and insurance, but the salaries of health care workers (including doctors) have not risen to the same extent as other costs. There are many more people working today in the United States compared to 1972, with 73 million people working then and more than 133 million working today, and this is largely due to the increase in the population. However, the percentage of people working today is also higher (64%) than it was in 1972 (60%).

There has been concern from politicians and others that many jobs are being taken from American workers by immigrants, but this does not appear to be as big a problem as some of our politicians would like us to believe. Of the 465 civilian occupations, only 4 are majority immigrant, and these 4 occupations account for less than 1 percent of the total U.S. workforce; even then, in these professions native-born Americans account for 47 percent of the workers in these jobs. Some jobs that are often thought to be largely immigrant are actually more often held by native-born Americans. For example, in these professions the percentage of native born Americans are:

- Maids and housekeepers—55 percent
- Taxi drivers and chauffeurs—58 percent
- Butchers and meat processors—63 percent
- Grounds maintenance workers—65 percent
- Construction workers—65 percent
- Porters, bellhops, and concierges—71 percent
- Janitors—75 percent

Most of the largely immigrant jobs are primarily but not exclusively lower-wage jobs that require little formal education. It is simply not true that immigrants are taking away jobs from American-born workers, although native-born workers who may be most affected are the less educated and poor. It must also be pointed out that not all high-immigrant occupations are in the low paying sector. For example, the following professions have quite a few immigrants: medical scientists (44%), software engineers (34%), physicians (27%), and chemists (25%). In these jobs it is the training, education, and experience that will lead to employment, so these jobs are not taken by immigrants over native-born people with the same credentials. It is also worth noting that there are quite a few politically important jobs that have very few immigrants; for example, reporters (10%), lawyers and judges (6%), and farmers/ranchers (3%).

SUMMARY AND CONCLUSION

Work and jobs in the United States and in most other parts of the world have changed so completely in the past century that someone from the early 20th century would not understand, believe, or even recognize the jobs that many people do today. Similarly, workers have changed, organizations and companies have changed, education has changed, laws and regulations have changed, and quite frankly almost everything in the world of work is far different than it was a century ago. Most Americans believe that the United States is the best place in the world to work, but the research evidence suggests that we have some room for improvement. According to Business Insider, the United States is not even in the top 10 for the countries with the best workers—in fact we are ranked 16th in the world for having the best workers. However, very similarly, the *Wall Street Journal* finds that in terms of how well workers are treated by employers, we also rank a disappointing 16th behind most European countries and many others as well. In fact, the International Trade Union Congress evaluated countries around the world in terms of their violations of worker rights and placed them in five categories from 1 (the best) to 5 (the worst). The United States was placed in category 4 because of 30 or more consistent and systematic violations of workers' rights, and we are in the same category as countries like Kenya.

Hopefully, as we learn more about workers, jobs, and labor needs, we will be in a position to do better at creating organizations and jobs that improve the quality of work, the quality of worker's lives, the quality and performance of organizations, and the betterment of society and the world in general. These may be lofty goals, but to aspire to less is not acceptable.

2

❖

Why: The Importance of Work in Our Lives

To determine some of the reasons why people work, it is important to first recognize the complexity of this issue. Of course, all people are different, and all people have various reasons and motives for doing the things that they do, but it is even more complicated than this. Not only do different people work for different reasons, but every individual works for a variety of reasons as well, which may change over time and even differ from one day to the next. For example, suppose that you take up a job because you need the money to survive; then you go to work and find that the paycheck is great; you also discover that you are working with some very nice and helpful people, and then the next day, your social needs are more important to you as you go to work than are the survival needs, which you now take for granted. The things that determine why people work will differ from person to person, from culture to culture, from generation to generation, and depending on a person's sex and other personal characteristics. With all of this in mind, we now must consider that every person will have multiple reasons why they work, and these reasons will change in importance and urgency over time and even within hours, moments, days, weeks, months, years, decades, and so on.

This may appear so hopelessly complex that it may seem that it would be impossible to ever try to figure out why people work. However, we do not want to get too pessimistic too quickly; there certainly are reasons why people work, and we will explore some of those things and how they affect people in the workplace. One of the things that people look for in determining why people work is "job satisfaction"; one would think that people are more likely to want to work if they like their job. There is something called "global job satisfaction," and that refers to a general sense that someone has about their job. Suppose you asked someone to tell you how they like their job on a 10-point scale, and they tell you that their feeling about their job is about a "6." This is an example of one very simplistic measure of global job satisfaction. However, when most people tell you about their feelings about their job, they will give more complicated answers; for example, "Well, I really like my coworkers, but my boss is a jerk; the salary is ok, but the benefits stink." These are examples of what we refer to as "job facet satisfaction," because we are reacting to different "facets" of our job. In reality, when researchers study job satisfaction in the workplace, they typically use very thorough and detailed questionnaires about various facets of jobs as well as more global measures, and then they calculate the job satisfaction globally and for different facets as well.

It seems very logical that if a person really likes his or her job, then that would certainly be one of the reasons why the person might work. However, the relationship between job satisfaction and different work outcomes is not as clear as it might appear. For example, many people have heard that a "happy worker is a productive worker," and this seems to make sense at first glance; unfortunately, it is not that simple. There are hundreds of studies on the relationship between job satisfaction and work performance, and the relationship is a weak but positive relationship—that is, job satisfaction is related to performance a little bit but not that much. Why would that be? If we think about it for a minute, it seems to make more sense. Job performance depends on many things that have nothing to do with job satisfaction. For example, does the person have the ability and skills to do the job well? Do they have the relevant support and equipment to do their job well? Are they adequately trained? These are all important questions about job performance, and therefore, a better way to think about the relationship between job performance and job satisfaction is the statement: "To the extent that other factors are held constant, the more someone likes their job the better their performance."

We also look at the relationship between job satisfaction and attendance, and here we have the same type of situation as we did with performance. Job satisfaction is only mildly related to attendance, but this too does not seem to make sense; if someone likes his or her job, would he or she not be more likely to go to work? Once again, there are complicating factors. Research has found that attendance is related to a wide variety of factors in addition to job satisfaction. For example, the things that determine attendance include a person's health, the presence of young children in the home, the weather, the availability of transportation, how far a person lives from work, and many others. To summarize the findings of a very large number of studies, it can be said that "to the extent that attendance is under the control of the employee, then job satisfaction is a good predictor of attendance."

There is one other factor that is clearly affected by job satisfaction, and that is voluntary turnover (when a person leaves his or her job for his or her own reasons). This is one factor where the relationship with job satisfaction is a little clearer. The research evidence does indicate that the more satisfied a person is with his or her job, the less likely he or she to leave it, and that does make very good sense. Therefore, it does seem that job satisfaction is one factor that is related to the reasons why a person would want to work, but like many other things, it is not a simple relationship. One other factor that is an important concern involves the relationship people have with their jobs and employers. As discussed earlier, there is not the loyalty between employer and employee that we found even in the recent past. Many workers today look at their job as just a paycheck and expect that their employers will probably lay them off anyway, so why even worry about job satisfaction.

However, there are many writers, researchers, and other professionals who keep emphasizing the importance of work and jobs being far more important to people than just a paycheck. Many feel that work should be an opportunity for a creative and social outlet for people that encourages and supports them in fulfilling some of their own goals and being productive and valuable employees. There is substantial research suggesting that there is real value in helping people find meaning and significance in their work. We know that finding meaning in one's work increases motivation, engagement in work, feelings of empowerment, career development, job satisfaction, individual performance, and feelings of personal fulfillment. It has also been found that finding meaning in one's work decreases absenteeism and work stress.

Work engagement means that workers are passionate about their work and strongly committed to their companies. In "The State of the American Workforce," the Gallup company found that only about 30 percent of the U.S. workforce is engaged in their work; the remaining 70 percent are either "not engaged" or "actively disengaged." These unengaged workers are not as productive, require more time and attention from management, and often undermine the accomplishments of others. These unengaged workers are more likely to steal from the company, negatively influence coworkers, miss workdays, and drive customers away. It is estimated that worker disengagement probably costs American companies $456–$500 billion/year. Very frequently, companies blame this disengagement on workers and see the solution as hiring people who will be more engaged. However, experience tells us that engagement is usually a worker's response to the way they feel that they are treated and valued by their organizations.

The rare workers who feel that they have a "higher calling" to their work are the most content—even if they are not well paid. For example, more than 80 percent of zookeepers have college educations, but on average, they make less than $25,000/year; and very interestingly, many of them report that they were "born to do this work." It is unfortunate that these well-educated and dedicated employees are taken advantage of with near-poverty-level salaries only because they love their work, but thankfully they are committed to their jobs and their organizations, and the people who visit the zoos and the zoo animals that benefit from their work are certainly grateful for these dedicated and engaged workers. Although college-educated zoo workers are more engaged in their jobs, it is not true that college-educated workers are generally more engaged in their jobs, and in fact they tend to be less engaged than workers with less education even though they are likely to make more money.

Companies that would like to have employees who are more engaged need to first look at the work environment and management practices. For example, employees respond very positively to having some authority in making decisions about the design of their work and how it is performed. They also like working in productive and positive groups and teams. Workers respond well to positive and supportive leadership and are more likely to respond to high expectations if they feel that they are valued and respected by superiors and coworkers. Workers are more likely to feel positive about their jobs and organizations when they trust their managers and the people around them, and they will be more committed to their organization when they feel that the organization cares about them. Companies today expect and need employees to be flexible and willing to learn new things, and as long as the expectations are clear, employees receive adequate training, and the amount of work expected in reasonable, employees usually respond very positively to these needs and expectations.

Employees like to have not only a sense of responsibility for their work but also the authority needed to fulfill these responsibilities, and in today's organizations, employees, supervisors, and lower-level managers usually have more responsibility than authority, which is very stressful and makes it more difficult for people to do their jobs well. Workers also like having a sense of control over the things that they have to do and the responsibilities that they have, but often this is not the case, and workers often feel that they have very little control over anything having to do with their job. Finally, most workers want a sense of belongingness in their work groups and organizations, but unfortunately, many companies feel that socialization other than work-related interaction is a waste of work time; however, the research evidence is that when people feel socially validated and involved with their work colleagues, they are more productive and more likely to be engaged with the organization.

In many work environments, there is a tendency for management to blame workers for performance and morale issues and the workers likewise tending to blame management for these problems. In most cases, it is unlikely that these types of issues will be solved by only one person or group trying to fix things—usually things do not get much better unless all of the people involved try to improve the situation. As mentioned earlier, if management notices some problems, they should try to discover why the problems exist, and then they should try to see what kinds of management solutions they might employ. On the other hand, when employees notice difficulties, they should look at things that they can do to improve the situation. For example, some of the things that workers can do include altering the tasks that they perform in order to make them more efficient and more enjoyable. They can also change some of their relationships in the workplace—we cannot make other people change, but we can change how we act, and sometimes we can also change whom we interact with. There are also techniques that psychologists can help people learn that enable them to use "cognitive restructuring" to change how they think about their job. This means that the person tries to find ways to think differently about his or her job. For example, suppose a worker was feeling discouraged about his or her job and that he or she might be trapped in that job forever. Another way to look at the situation is to think, "I may not want to do this job for the rest of my life, but it is paying me a salary, so I can help support my family, and if I work hard and do a good job, I will get a better raise and hopefully be considered for a promotion." Only thinking about things will not usually change them, but if we let our actions follow our thoughts, then we will begin to see some differences.

REASONS WHY PEOPLE WORK

Survival

The one motive for people working that has been true for the entire history of humanity is survival. The need to provide nourishment, safety, shelter, and social structure has very likely always been a part of the human experience. Work was one thing that people could do to help them survive. By needing to eat and drink, people had to find ways to provide for themselves. Since there were no stores to go to and no plumbing to bring water into the house, they had to find food and bring it back; further, they had to find water and find ways to make it available when it was needed. It was also important that people were available to care for the young, old, and ill or injured.

Human beings are social animals and have always had the inclination to live in groups for support and protection. By living in groups, it would be very likely that people would begin to move into different "jobs" to take care of all the various tasks of living, but the basic reason for all of this was survival, because if these different tasks were not fulfilled, people would die. It is not an exaggeration to say that if people had not learned how to work at the earliest stages of human society, we as a species would never have survived and evolved. If we examine all of human history, we can find many different changes that were important in understanding how people lived and developed over time. However, the history of work and working is a very good way to follow the progress of human society and to understand how people lived and why they did the things that they did.

In the workplace today, many people do not think of basic survival as one of the reasons why they work, but it is as true today as it was in the past, but it is much more complex than it was in previous eras. Of course, we have jobs to make money, and we need money to pay rent or buy houses, and we need it to buy groceries and supplies; money pays for the means of transportation, for medical and dental care, and for our clothing and shoes so that we are protected against the weather and other conditions. Money is also needed to pay for roads and bridges, and we pay for that through taxes, which really means that we are paying the government so that they can hire people to do the jobs that are necessary to build and fix the roads and bridges that we need. Taxes also pay for firefighters, police, military, teachers, and government workers, all of whom do jobs that are important for the rest of us to have the safe and comfortable lives that we want. Having jobs provides ways for us to meet our personal and community needs that allow us to survive and prosper.

Looking at work in today's world also points out some of the ways in which work is directly related to survival in the most basic sense. People in many parts of the world, including the United States, do not have enough to eat; they lack basic medical care; they do not live in safe and secure environments; and they worry about surviving daily. Although many people today earn enough so that they do not worry about the basics of survival, it is still a fundamentally important issue for millions of people in this country and around the world. To worry about things like job satisfaction is irrelevant to people who do not even have a job; to be concerned about a person being engaged in his or her job when the job involves working in terrible and unsafe conditions and barely pays the person enough money for food and housing makes very little sense. Clearly, even if we do not often think about jobs as necessary for survival, this is still the most basic reason why people work. Any society needs to insure that there are opportunities for all people to work so that they can take an active hand in their own survival, but too often today, people do not think of the survival of others as being any of their business. However, since the main reason why people work is to survive, we should make it a social and cultural priority to educate and train people so that they can get jobs and work to support themselves and to contribute to the support of society as a whole. This may sound unrealistically idealistic, but to hope for and expect less takes society down roads that will not lead to the kind of world that most of us would like to live in.

Need for Control and Power

This may sound negative, like some people are "control freaks" or "power mongers," but the reality is that all people have needs for control and power. Of course, some people have extremely high needs, and others may have somewhat low needs, but everyone has these needs in one way or another. It is easy to understand where these needs come from, and it appears that there is a genetic basis for having these needs. This makes perfectly good sense when we consider the fact that without a need to take control and get things done, the species probably would not have survived, and therefore, our humanoid ancestors who were more competent and got things done would be more likely to find a mate and reproduce, thus establishing and reinforcing a genetic predisposition regarding control and power. Let us also be aware of what these needs mean—control needs have to do with being competent and effective in one's physical and social environment. Some people may seem to overdo this type of need, and when this happens, others may feel uncomfortable or even resentful of the controlling person seeming to always want things their way. However, for most people, exercising one's control needs does not usually result in "stepping on other's toes" or ignoring their position, but rather appropriately taking control of things in their environment over which they can and should control.

Similarly, the need for power does not mean that a person wants or needs to be powerful and to order people around and always manipulate others to do their bidding. Certainly, there are those who seem to have an exaggerated need for power, and sometimes this need can be very destructive (e.g., Hitler, Stalin, Mao). However, the need for power in most people simply means that they want to have an impact on situations or other people and to do something to make a difference. Expressed this way, it seems less negative and can even seem like power might not be such a bad thing.

When we consider the reasons why people might want or need to work, it does seem clear that needs for control and power would be part of the reasons why they work and have jobs. If it is true that these needs are found in all people to greater or lesser degrees, then it is reasonable to consider how these needs might be important for workers in their jobs. In fact, there is a substantial amount of research that indicates that people do want and need for feeling some control over their jobs and how they do them. Frequently, managers and supervisors assume that workers are usually lazy and will not do much of anything unless they absolutely have to. Managers and supervisors who are overly controlling and do not let the employees have much of a voice in how they do their jobs will often find that their subordinates will show very little initiative and do not accomplish very much unless they are ordered and controlled to do things. However, if you ask these employees why they do not perform more and why they do not show any initiative, many of them will say things like, "Why bother? Whatever I do is wrong anyway, and if I try to initiate anything, I get yelled at." Of course, there are some employees who are just lazy, but that truly is not most employees. In fact, one study found that employees frequently would like to do more in their jobs than they are allowed to, but their supervisors will not let them. Supervisors will usually respond with something like, "That is not my employees—mine won't do anything if I don't stay right on top of them." So which is right? Probably both. There are some workers who will not do anything if they are not told to do so, but research and systematic observation tell us that this is only a minority of workers. It appears to be true that given the chance to have some input and control over how to do their jobs, many employees will actually do more work and do it better than if they are always told what to do and how to do it. How then does a manager keep control of worker behavior? The answer is actually simple: be clear in your expectations; set goals; give feedback; recognize success; and correct mistakes giving the person a chance to learn from his or her errors and improve.

Power and control needs are a basic part of the psychological makeup of all people. To recognize this in the workplace and find ways to encourage healthy ways to meet these needs will lead to higher levels of performance and happier employees. If this is so clear and backed up by solid research, why then does it not happen more frequently in the workplace? Primarily because managers and supervisors, in trying to do their own jobs as best as they can, are often afraid of giving up their own control for fear that the employees will not do their jobs as well as they are needed to. However, by managers and employees working together and listening to one another, it is surprising how well these needs can not only work to the advantage of the individual workers but also help managers do a better job, both of which will also lead to improved organizational performance.

Work as a Means of Gaining Success and Comfort

In our culture, people frequently talk about "the important things in life" like health, family, friends, being happy with our life, and other such things. However, there is no doubt that we tend to judge success by what kind of a job someone has, how famous he or she is, and by how much money he or she makes. Whether we think this is a good thing or not, it is certainly the way that many people feel and act. It is easy to see how making money will help people lead and live a more comfortable life. However, it is probably true that most people like having money because of the prestige it brings to them, the control it gives them over others, as well as the comforts it provides them. The fact that most Americans are significantly in debt is probably a good indicator of how much we want and apparently need money to have the kind of lifestyle that many people aspire to. Since an increasingly smaller percentage of the population is classified as rich or wealthy, the middle class is shrinking, and the ranks of the working poor, and those in abject poverty, are significantly increasing, it seems clear that having money to improve one's quality of life will become an increasingly difficult thing for most people. For example, currently, the richest 1 percent in the United States holds about 38 percent of all privately held wealth in the United States, whereas the bottom 90 percent holds 73 percent of all debt. According to the *New York Times*, the "richest 1 percent in the United States now own more wealth than the bottom 90 percent." It was also recently announced that

80 richest people in the world have more wealth that the poorest 50 percent of the entire world combined. Think about that—80 rich people have more money than the lower half of all of the people on the earth. Although having money is still one of the things that people think of as an indicator of success, it will become increasingly difficult for most "normal" people to become wealthy or even financially comfortable.

Regardless of these financial concerns, it still remains true that people look at their jobs as one of the primary ways to be seen as successful and having a good salary and benefits should improve the comforts and quality of one's life. Perhaps we might be more concerned about the huge numbers of people in the United States and around the world who do not have good jobs or an adequate income and frequently have no access to benefits like health care or pensions. Thus, it is true that many people see their jobs as providing success and comfort in their lives, but the other side of that coin is that there are many more people seeing an inferior or nonexistent job as evidence of their poor quality of life, the absence of success, and very little in the way of comforts in their life.

The Social Contract

In social philosophy, the idea of the social contract reflects the actual or implicit agreement between citizens and the governing person or body that the people will give up some of their rights and freedoms in exchange for protection and for the provision of services. Earlier we discussed the "psychological contract" between employer and employee, and this is very similar. The social contract is a little more specific in that it does refer to the employee giving up some rights and following directions and orders that the employer requires or requests in exchange for a salary and benefits, appropriate training, supplies (as well as support and equipment) necessary to do one's job, and reasonable job security.

If we look at the workplace today, it is not difficult to see how the social contract is not as balanced and equitable as it might have been in the past, and it is one of the reasons why the relationship between employers and employees is not as strong and stable as it was in the recent past. At this point, many employers feel that if an employee does not do everything that is expected, then he or she can just be fired and someone else can be found to do the job. Employees, on the other hand, often feel that if they do not like their job or employer, they will just quit and find another job. There are some troubling consequences to this state of affairs, and they are not to the advantage of workers or companies. Employees who change jobs frequently are not as attractive to potential employers because they fear that there is either something wrong with the employee that employers do not like or that the person is not stable enough to settle down and stick with a job. Further, when people change jobs frequently, they lose seniority, they often have to start over in their benefits (like vacation time), they do not get as close to coworkers, and therefore, their work groups are not as important to them, and if their organizations have pension plans, this may disrupt their accumulation of retirement savings.

When companies turn over employees frequently, it may look like they are saving money because they are firing people with higher salaries and replacing them with workers at a lower salary level. However, this does not account for the costs of turnover, which is very expensive. Unfortunately, most employers do not consider some of the subtle or hidden costs of turnover when they look at the expenses. For example, "hard costs" of turnover include the direct costs of advertising for jobs, recruiting and interviewing employees, and paying people to interview and process prospective and new employees. Also, if they fire people, they may also have to pay unemployment insurance, and if the high-stress environment they create with frequent layoffs and dismissals starts to affect people, they can expect to have increased lost work time as well as higher workers' compensation claims for illness and stress-related problems. Another thing that employers usually do not consider is the lost productivity when turnover increases. If you have an existing employee worker at a certain level and that employee leaves or is fired, then his or her productivity goes down to zero where it will stay until a new employee comes in. After the new worker is on the job, he or she will not perform at the same level as the older employee—at least not initially. By the time the new worker is as productive as the person he or she replaced, there is a period of decreased productivity that will never be replaced. It is obvious that if a company has high turnover rates, then all of these expenses will increase dramatically, and this is certainly not a good thing for any business.

When one looks at the social contract and similar concepts, it is easy to see how each side of this could easily blame the other side, and then, of course, nothing changes, and the situation does not improve. The only way that this type of condition will get better is when both sides look at it differently, take responsibility for their own actions, and start to do things differently. If employers start treating employees better and more fairly and if employees start taking their jobs more seriously and try to be more conscientious and productive, it is very probable that the companies will start being more successful and the workers will be happier and perform at higher levels. As simple as this sounds, however, the two sides to these problems have shown little interest in changing the ways that they are doing things, and of course, "if nothing changes—nothing changes."

Work and Social Connectedness

Most people who have jobs outside their own home spend more time with their colleagues at work than they do with their family and friends—particularly if we do not count time sleeping. Therefore, for many of us, our work group is an important social reference group—this means that the people we work with are important social connections for us. Many people socialize with their work colleagues, which makes these relationships even more important, even for people who do not "hang out" with coworkers; the work group is still an important group in our lives. When workers report good relationships with coworkers, this will be reflected in higher levels of job satisfaction, less absenteeism, and lower turnover. It also leads to workers reporting less stress and fewer stress-related health and mental health issues. This is particularly true when workers report having good relationships with the supervisors and managers. Conversely, research demonstrates that poor supervision and inadequate managers are one of the main sources of stress reported by workers. Thus, if the social relationships at work (with both coworkers and superiors) are reported as positive by employees, they are more satisfied and productive and less likely to voluntarily leave their job.

This points out a very interesting development in the modern workplace that we are beginning to recognize as an issue. It is not uncommon for many workers to "telecommute" or to work from home at least part of the time. In fact, virtual workplaces are becoming much more common, and this is when workers do not come into the office at all but will work from home or via computer/tablet and rarely interact directly with their coworkers or bosses. This type of work has dramatically changed the workplace and often with very good results. It cuts down transportation time and costs, lets people work in their own space and time, and cuts down on management time and resources as well as eliminates the need for people to have on-site offices. In fact, we could put together a work team from all over the world, and they could work together using computer-mediated communication systems and even work "asynchronously," which means they can work together but not necessarily at the same time.

As important a development as telecommuting and virtual work teams have become, these advances are not without complications. Probably the main problem with these types of work is the substantial change in the role of socialization at work. Regardless of what people think, texting, emailing, tweeting, and the like are not the same thing as talking directly to someone. There are not the same social cues, body language, and other nonverbal communication subtleties that cannot be replaced with emoticons or other cute little visual symbols. Not only do we lose rich communication, but we are also finding that with people working remotely, they do not have as much connection with their work group, do not interact with their supervisor as much, do not feel as committed to their group and organization, are more likely to leave and find another job, and do not have as much job satisfaction. There is no question but that working remotely and having the virtual office is here to stay, and they can be very good options. However, managing remotely is not the same as managing in an office, and we have to find ways to educate and train managers and employees as to how to optimize performance and satisfaction in workers who are not in the office. We are starting to see some new research literature in this area, and hopefully, we will find better ways to deal with workers more effectively in the new work environment.

We know that the work group and work environment are very important social experiences for most people and that for people to enjoy and be productive at work and for organizations to be efficient and effective, we must find ways to take advantage of people's social needs for their own benefit and for the improvement of their companies. Rather than seeing the difficulties in the realm as hopeless, everyone, including companies, executives, workers, and labor unions, need to see these problems as opportunities for improvement and work together to accomplish these goals. By working together, there is a chance of actually improving the situation for everyone.

Work as a Means of Self-Determination and Identity

"Self-determination" refers to things that a person may do that will establish him or her as an active and self-controlled individual who is able to do the things that he or she needs or wants to do. For all of us, the idea of "freedom" refers to the "state of being" where we have many options for things that we can do, and the ability to choose among those options. Therefore, to the extent that we have opportunities from which to select our activities, and we can access and act upon our preferences, then we are "free." Many of us who live in countries where freedom and liberty are taken for granted do not realize how important self-determination really is and how that is something very rare and often unknown in other parts of the world.

Why, then, would work be important for self-determination? One of the things that is very obvious in any society is that people with better jobs and higher income have more "freedom" in the sense that there are many things that they are able to do that many of the rest of us cannot afford or have access to. To be able to come and go as we please, to travel wherever and whenever we want, to live in a home with many advantages, to go to school or college wherever we choose, to drive the car of our dreams—all of these things may be open to anyone if they have the money or the influence to actually have access to them. Without question, one's station in life in any country will determine how much freedom that he or she actually has. Some might assert that in a "free" country like the United States, everyone is free to do whatever they want to do, but it is equally clear that I might be free to buy a $10 million home and a $500,000 car, but since I cannot afford either of those things, the freedom to do something that I am not able to do anyway is not really freedom at all.

Since much of how we spend our lives depends on the resources and opportunities that are available to us, our job will have quite a bit to do with the extent to which we can determine our own activities and the life that we actually live on a day-to-day basis. Income is certainly an important determinant of the range of activities that we are able to be involved with, and the more money we have, the more things we can afford to buy and to do. Because "self-determination" relies on our being able to "determine" what we want to do, it is easy to see how money can help, but this is also a somewhat complicated issue. Some people get so caught up in making money and then seem to need even more money that they get trapped in the "rat race" of getting more "stuff" and needing to make more money to buy more "stuff," and on and on it seems to go. In these types of situations, the money starts limiting what a person can do because he or she seems to have to spend more of his or her time to make more money to try to keep up with his or her new spending patterns. In fact, we can all think of people who do not have much money but seem to have very high levels of self-determination and are able to do the things that are most important to them, and often this does not require a lot of money. However, even then the person's job will have a lot to do with his or her self-determination. The person still must be able to support himself or herself and provide the necessities of life even if these are very basic. If a person has a job that allows him or her to support himself or herself as well as gives him or her the time and opportunities to do the things that he or she needs to do to feel fulfilled, then this is an example of how a job can provide the chance for self-determination without having to depend primarily on the financial resources that the person's salary provides.

Another situation where the job provides opportunities for self-determination is when the job itself allows degrees of freedom and opportunity that most people do not have. For example, a police officer on a call, and even if he or she is in civilian clothes and in a private car, can run red lights and speed without worrying about getting a ticket. Similarly a doctor on an emergency can park wherever he or she needs to without fear of getting fined. I am sure that you can think of some professions where the job gives people rights and privileges that most people do not have. This is another example of how one's job can provide opportunities for self-determination.

Probably the most important aspect of self-determination is how that links to a person's "identity." By identity we are referring to how a person is viewed and "identified" as an individual by other people. "Self-identity" refers to how we perceive and identify ourselves. When we are introduced to someone we do not know, there are some very basic questions we ask of one another. For example, "Where do you live?" "Do you have a family?" "What do you do?" All of these questions refer to elements of a person's identity, and it is very clear that part of our identities is based on our "job" or what we do. Being a student is the job of most young people, and even though that job does not come with a salary, it does have responsibilities and expectations that are like having a job. Even if a person does not have a job, this is still part of his or her identity and has something to do with his or her ability to exert self-determination. For example, unemployed, disabled, and retired are examples of elements of identity for people who may not actually have a job. Some people think that being a homemaker is not a real job, but if you look at how a woman or man who is primarily a homemaker spends her or his time, it is very clear that this is a job—a very important job. However, this is not a job that comes with a paycheck, but it is very important and is clearly part of a person's identity, and if you consider what it would cost to pay someone else to provide these housekeeping and childcare tasks, then it is very clear that this "job" has financial impact.

In summary, in many different ways, work and jobs are very important in allowing a person to be able to determine what he or she does and how he or she spends his or her time—that is, the person's work is important for his or her self-determination. Similarly, work also provides a very important part of our identity—how we are perceived by others and how we perceive ourselves. Even people without jobs have different kinds of work that they have to do to support themselves and survive, and this too is part of their identity.

Work as a Way of Structuring Individual and Social Life

People do not usually think of work as an important element in how we actually organize and structure our time. For example, what determines how you spend your time in a given day? There are certain biological requirements that must be met—we have to sleep, we have to eat, we have to drink, and we have to take care of other biological imperatives like elimination, but these things do not take up all or even most of our time. What then are the other things that we have to do during the day? Some people have jobs and have to go to work, and they usually have a fixed schedule as to when they are supposed to be at work and how long they have to stay. Other people may be caregivers and have responsibility for children or others who depend upon them. In this case, it may be other people's needs that determine how and when we spend our time, but still there is a way of determining how our time is spent. If we take all of the mandatory things that are required of us in life, including jobs or other types of work like school, caregiving, or self-care, this still leaves time that we will fill with other activities like rest and recreation as well as things like sports, music, exercise, and socialization.

For most people, their work is a major determinant of how they structure all of the rest of their time. Even the time that we sleep may depend on our work. Some people work on different shifts because of their job, and if they have to work at night, then they may actually have to sleep during the day, and some people actually like and prefer these different types of job schedules. All people have some type of work that they must do—even if that work is not a job. The things that we have to do to support ourselves and to provide for ourselves are a big part of how we structure our time. Even people who are disabled or retired still have things that they have to do to take care of themselves and their responsibilities, and these activities will determine how we spend at least part of our time.

Most of us do not think about how important structure is in our lives, and thus we typically just take it for granted as if it were something fixed or essential like gravity. Structure makes it possible for us to have some sense of predictability and control in our lives so that we can get done the things that must be done, take care of the responsibilities required of us, support and care for the people and organizations that depend on us, and (hopefully) to have some time for recreation and relaxation and to do some of the fun things that we enjoy. Without structure, life would be chaotic and without a foundation and sense of purpose. Sometimes it seems like all of the things we have to do just get in the way of doing all of the things that we really want to do. To be able to go to bed when you want to, to get up when you want to, to eat what you want and when you want to, and to play games/watch TV/listen to music/go to movies/ hang out with friends or go shopping whenever you want sound like a life many people would really enjoy. However, who is going to pay for all of these privileges? Parents? Certainly many parents are willing to support their children to do many of these things, but this support usually depends on things like the child going to school, taking care of their other responsibilities, doing their chores, or working a part-time job. The privilege and freedom to do the things we want to do come with a price, and this means that all of us at some point in our lives have to learn how to structure our time so that we get the things done that we need to get done in order to have time to do all of the things that we really want to do. Also, when people grow up and leave home, most do not have families so wealthy that they will never have to work at a regular job, and therefore when people move out on their own (even if they have some help getting started), they have to find a job that pays them enough to take care of where they live, transportation, expenses, food, and the like. Now, their time is structured very differently, and they will usually need to structure their time around a job that provides the income that they need to support their new and independent lifestyle.

Perhaps the best example of how important work is for structuring our time is what happens to people when they retire. When a person is very used to structuring their lives around a job, the lack of a job can be very disorienting and even upsetting. When you depend on the job to determine when and how much you sleep, when you have free days off, when you take a vacation, and how you spend most of your time during the day, then not having this structure can be very problematic for many people. Research demonstrates that depression is very common among retired people and disabled people as well, and part of the reason for this is disorganizing effect the lack of daily structure has on their lives as well as the sense of lack of purpose when they do not have a job that helps define who they are as a person. Interestingly, this problem of depression following retirement is more frequently a problem for men than women, but this makes good sense when you think about it. In the United States, men may work more hours outside the home than most women, but most women do far more work in the home and usually have most of the responsibility for childcare—this is not true in all families, but it is still true in most. Thus, women usually have more experience in structuring their time outside of work, and therefore, even if retirement is stressful for them as well, it may not be as disorganizing for them as it may be for many men.

Structure is also very important for people's social lives as well as their personal and individual lives. Many people socialize with people from their neighborhood, friends they went to school with or lived near, family, and coworkers. We usually spend more time during the workdays with our colleagues at work than we do with any other group of people with whom we spend time socially. It is hardly surprising that many people build good friendships at work since these are people we spend time with on most days and with whom we have many things in common because we work in the same place and often in similar jobs. It is also true that work often includes social opportunities like a common lunch or break time and a place where people can socialize while at work. There may also be activities sponsored at work like clubs, sports, trips, and the like where people can get together and socialize. When people have friends over to their home or have parties, it is often people from work who are invited—even if the guests are not all work colleagues, they are still frequently part of the guest list.

Clearly work is an important part of everyone's life, and one of the reasons why it is so important is the structure it provides for our personal and social life. This is easy to see when a person's work is organized around a job, but it is also true if a person's work happens to be at home or caring for others. As extreme an example as this might be, work is also very important to homeless people who may not even have a job. They still need to find places to sleep or keep out of the weather, they still have to take care of their basic needs, and they still need to eat and drink—probably most of their "free time" during the day is some type of work that they do to find ways to meet their basic needs and to survive.

SUMMARY AND CONCLUSION

In this chapter, we have explored some of the reasons why people work, and although we covered most of the main reasons, there are probably many others that may be unusual or even unique for some people or groups. Clearly, survival is historically and evolutionarily the most important reason why people have worked throughout history, but as humans have progressed throughout the eras, their lives have become much more complex, the motives that drive them have become more varied, and the reasons why they work have become more complicated as well.

Some of the other reasons we discussed for why people work included the need for power and control, which simply means that all people have a need to be in control of things in their lives and the need to make a difference for themselves and those who are important to them, and work is certainly one way in which these needs can be fulfilled. Similarly, work is one mechanism for gaining success and comfort in our lives, and for most people, their job is the main thing that determines the quality of their lives and their standard of living. Of course, very rich people have so much money that the only job they really have is to make sure that the money continues to come in and provide the things that they have come to expect from life; however, that is certainly not the case for most people.

One reason for working that is not as obvious is the social contract. This refers to the understood "agreement" that people have with society and others that implies that in exchange for working, they will have the benefits of living in a group that supports and protects one another. In every social group in the world, there appears to be this unwritten agreement that determines the expectations a group has of its members and the kinds of "work" that people will do to support themselves and the group. It is also true that in every group, there may be people who for various reasons are not able to fulfill this social contract, and the group then must either decide to eliminate those individuals from the group or may decide that the reasons that the person cannot fulfill his or her end of the contract are valid, and the group will agree to support those who are unable to support themselves or the group. Sociologists, anthropologists, and historians have studied people throughout history and have found that the social contract is one of the fundamental bases for human survival and prosperity and is unquestionably one of the main reasons why people work.

Since people spend so much of their time working, it is obvious that the people with whom they work become a very important "social reference group." This means that work groups and colleagues are groups that are important in the social life of most people, and this too is another reason why people work. If you ask people what they like or do not like about their jobs, their friends and relationships at work are usually one of the factors that they will mention. Similarly, people work because their jobs and the organizations they work for become a part of their personal identity and how they see themselves. Their jobs also give them a sense that they have the capacity and opportunity for self-determination, which means that they have ways to express themselves, impact the world around them, and actually fulfill the identity that they are forming.

Finally, and very importantly, work is one of the most important things for a person to help them structure their personal and social life. Work helps bring order, predictability, and purpose to our daily lives even if we get tired of working so much and working so hard. Many other countries are moving to shorter workweeks, more flexible schedules, longer vacations, and more liberal leave time. Hopefully, we can find more ways for workers to be productive, satisfied with their jobs, and have a balanced and rewarding life.

3

❖

How: The Positive and Negative Effects of Work

Having looked at work throughout history, it is obvious that work in one form or another has always been a part of our lives. This does suggest that there are some things about work that are important and even necessary for humans. In this chapter, we will examine some of the positive and negative elements of work and particularly how some of the changes in the world and the workplace today will impact workers, managers, and society at large.

On the positive side, work helps us survive by giving us the resources necessary to feed, clothe, and house ourselves and our families. Most people also like the sense of purpose and accomplishment that work provides, and this certainly gives a greater sense of meaning to our lives. Work also provides opportunities for social interaction and dealing with nonfamily people that makes our social life richer and more significant. Many people also truly enjoy their work and look forward to accomplishing their jobs and being recognized and appreciated for what they do. Work also helps us structure our time in ways that make us more efficient and organized. Although work takes time away from other activities that we might enjoy, by making us more mindful of our time, it makes it possible for us to plan in such a way as to be able to do some of the other things that we enjoy.

However, work has some negative factors as well, and when we hear people complaining about their jobs, this will give some idea as to the kinds of negative elements that are found in work. Work of any sort requires energy—even "mental" work uses energy, and whenever we use energy, this will eventually make us tired, and it means that we also need to stop and rest. Some jobs are more physically demanding and may use much more physical energy, and it is very clear that these types of jobs are tiring and might take a toll on the worker physically. Other jobs are more mentally exhausting, and in some ways, that might even seem more fatiguing to the person doing the work.

In a similar vein, some jobs are dangerous and may lead to injury or death. We often think of jobs like being in the military as being the most dangerous, and although the men and women in our nation's service put themselves on the line for us daily, there are many other jobs that are also dangerous as well. Police are in situations daily in which they can be injured or killed, and we are seeing examples of this in the news much more frequently in recent years. However, being a firefighter in some ways is more dangerous than being in the military or in the police if we look at the frequency of injury and death, and these people risk their lives every time they have a call.

Some of the other jobs that are very dangerous include things like being a farmer—this might surprise you, but it is true. Working on a farm means working with large machines and equipment that are often very dangerous. Farmers also work with livestock, and sometimes that can be dangerous as well; it is not surprising, then, that working on a farm is a very hazardous profession. Another dangerous job might also be surprising, and that is being a taxi driver. Because they often work alone at night and carry money, they are frequently the victims of violence at work and usually because of robbery. We also see some dangerous jobs on TV like being a North Sea crab fisherman or an ice road trucker, and these jobs can certainly be risky as well.

Other obviously dangerous jobs include things like being a boxer, NFL football player, mixed martial arts competitor, or an X Games participant. However, these jobs are ones that people choose to be involved with, and they know the risk but decide to accept the risk in exchange for the fame and money that they might receive. It is also true that society does not depend on any of these careers for survival—although we might enjoy watching or participating in them, we do not truly need them; these are "optional" jobs.

A primary issue about work that most people feel is a negative factor is that it takes us away from our families and others that we would like to spend time with and gives us less time to do some of the other things that we enjoy. Of course, by working, this gives us the financial resources to be able to do some of the other things that we like to do, but it still takes time away from those people and things we look forward to. Interestingly, for most people, retirement means that they no longer must work, and in this sense, retirement (not working) is the reward for spending most of one's life working! The dream for most people who retire is that they can now spend their time doing the things that they truly want to do. Unfortunately, in recent years, we have seen pensions eroded or eliminated, Social Security threatened, and people facing retirement with fewer resources to enjoy their time away from their job. Another negative aspect of work is that some people may have jobs that they really do not like but cannot afford to quit; they may be stuck looking at a lifetime of work doing something they dislike and just counting the days until they retire. This sounds like a very dismal way to spend one's life, but it is unfortunately not a rare condition.

One of the most important negative factors in work is stress, and this is the main source of workers' compensation claims today. This means that more people are taken out of work more frequently for stress-related problems than for any other injury or medical condition; this says a lot about the nature of the work environment today. There are numerous sources of stress at work, including the type of work one does, as well as things like poor working conditions, being inadequately paid, being treated poorly by supervisors or managers, and interpersonal conflict with coworkers or others at work—factors that can and do produce work stress.

Another stressful negative factor at work is prejudice and discrimination. Although many feel that these issues are things of the past, racism, sexism, ageism, and other forms of discrimination are still very much a part of the workplace and society today. We are even seeing discrimination against people because of their religion, and this is truly unfortunate in a country that was settled by Europeans who were seeking religious freedom. Of course, Americans also have the heritage of a Constitution that only referred to the men in society—women were not even allowed to vote or hold office. In fact, although many do not realize this, the original Constitution protected slavery to satisfy those states that economically depended on slavery to work on the plantations to harvest cotton and tobacco primarily, both of which were huge cash crops. Although things may be somewhat better today for some groups, it may be getting worse for others. Certainly, opportunities for women are better today than in the past, but research and experience still tell us that there is a "glass ceiling" that makes it more difficult for women to rise through the ranks to the highest levels in organizations, and women only make 77 cents to each dollar a man makes in the same job—things may be better than in the past, but we still have a way to go; discrimination and prejudice are still very much with us even today.

SOME OF THE POSITIVE AND NEGATIVE ASPECTS OF JOBS AND CAREERS TODAY

Jobs

Many people think that jobs are simply what people do at work, but although that might be part of the picture, it is not quite that simple. Think about what organizations do—they have products or services that they produce or provide (the outputs), and they have resources that they need to produce these products and services (the inputs). The processes that happen in the organization are the work that converts the inputs into outputs. Jobs represent how the organization's work is divided up so that the correct processes are efficiently transforming the inputs into usable and valuable outputs—valuable in that they are meeting the needs of the relevant customer or end user. After the jobs are defined appropriately and the work is divided in a meaningful and effective way, people are assigned to the various jobs so that the work is completed and the outputs achieved. This may sound simple, but it is not; in fact, you may need to read this paragraph several times before it makes sense, but when you get it, you will have a much better understanding of what jobs really are.

We often hear that jobs are changing, but with a better understanding of what jobs are, it is easy to see how all the changes we talked about earlier will impact the inputs, processes, and output requirements for all organizations, and therefore, the jobs will change as well. If the jobs change, then what people will need to do at work will change too. Perhaps one of the biggest things affecting jobs today is how quickly jobs are changing and how adaptable employees must be to keep up with the changes they face. A few years ago, one would not have thought that people like a salesperson in a department store, a car mechanic, a teacher, or a checkout clerk in a supermarket would all need to be technologically sophisticated and computer literate just to do their jobs, but if you watch these people at work now, you quickly see how important it is to be technically competent to do these jobs effectively. Further, since the technology we now use changes so quickly, about the time we feel that we have finally conquered our new phone, computer, tablet, and the like, they come out with a new version or new software, and we have to learn something new—this is true at work as well, and technical training is now a big part of what many organizations have to do continually to train new employees and to keep existing employees up to date with the latest technical changes. For many employees, these types of job changes might be a challenge and something that is very positive, but for others these new job requirements place considerable stress on the individual employee because they may not have the technical background to easily learn these new skills and to do the work that is now required for the job.

Jobs used to be determined by the "job description," which outlined the responsibilities, skills, tasks, and activities that an employee was expected to do. As mentioned earlier, it is rare today that organizations have accurate and updated job descriptions that define the jobs of most employees; this is because things usually change faster than the organization can officially modify all the relevant job descriptions. Today it is more important to make sure that goals and expectations for each employee in each job are clarified at least on an annual basis and more frequently if changes dictate the need for modification. In fact, if the supervisor or manager is clear in his or her expectations and the employee and his or her superior collaboratively set goals that match the expectations, the employee's performance evaluations can and should be based on these goals and expectations, which makes the whole process of feedback and evaluation much clearer and beneficial for the worker and for the organization. There is ample research evidence and experience that indicate how helpful it is to use goal setting as a way of determining criteria that can be used to evaluate performance for routine feedback and for formal performance evaluation. Even though goal setting is and can be very helpful for employees, it still depends on how it is used, and sometimes it may be a negative factor. For example, what if the goals are unrealistic or even unethical? This could be a real problem. Holding people accountable to accomplish goals that are unattainable is stressful and unfair, and asking them to do things that are unethical or even illegal is clearly wrong.

One difference in jobs today is how many different types of skills are required for employees in each job. Historically, labor unions were very strict about what a worker should be expected to do, and they could not be required to do a job that was not part of their job description. The reason for this was to prevent companies from eliminating jobs by making workers do part of someone else's job, which would cost jobs and unfairly expect workers to do more than they should have to do. As important as this basic idea was, it is probably unrealistic in today's world of work to expect jobs to be defined as precisely as they were in the past, and given the nature of work and jobs today, most jobs will expect workers to be more flexible and broadly trained than in the past, and the expectations of them at work might change frequently depending on the needs of the organization. This would not have happened in the past, but it is simply the way jobs are today, and most employers expect their employees to be able to adapt to those types of expectations. Thus, having employees who are broadly trained, flexible, adaptable, and willing to keep improving their skills and learn new things is very desirable for many organizations. This is one reason many organizations say that they want younger employees because they tend to be well informed technically and more flexible and willing to do many different things at work. However, it is also true that older employees, who are more experienced, know the organization and their job very well, and who are also willing to learn and adapt, may be laid off or fired so that younger employees can be hired. However, since most research demonstrates that more experienced and senior employees are almost always more productive than younger employees, one must question the real motives of the organizations that unfairly eliminate older employees in the name of getting "new blood." It is more likely that they can hire younger employees much more cheaply than paying a fair rate for the older workers. However, although this might seem to make sense financially, it is not very compelling when we look at the higher productivity for older workers.

It is obvious that jobs today are very different than they were even a few decades ago. Given the impact of globalization and technological change, it is very likely that jobs will be much more loosely defined in the future since individual jobs will change often and sometimes rapidly, and this will have an influence on most if not all jobs in the future. This reality will bring both positive and negative aspects into the jobs of the future, and how we deal with these issues will determine just how these effects will develop.

Careers

A topic that is very much related to jobs is "careers." Certainly, a career will involve a job, but it is much more than that. It also implies that a person is committed to a certain occupational path upon which the individual will be involved over time. Often, we think of careers that involve professions like doctor or lawyer, but they can involve other things like sales, being a mechanic, or many other things. Career implies training, expertise, and/or education to prepare for a long-term commitment to a path that goes beyond just having a job.

Since it seems clear that jobs have changed quite a bit in the past few years, it would seem logical to expect that careers will change as well. The old idea of getting a job with a company or organization, working for them for 20–30 years (or more), getting a nice retirement party with the "gold watch," receiving a fair and reasonable pension, and living comfortably through the "golden years" is not typical of workers' experiences or expectations these days. Job security is truly outdated in many organizations, and since so few people belong to unions these days, there is not much that requires companies to retain employees any longer than they want to—and many do not. As pointed out earlier, older workers are more efficient and more productive in most jobs, but since they also make more money, many companies think it is better to use less experienced and less productive workers and keep workers' salaries down. That only makes sense financially if you look at short-term financial savings, but most evidence suggests that this is not a good long-term approach; however, it is so tempting to find quick and easy ways to cut costs that layoffs, terminations, and early retirements are more often the rule than the exception.

Obviously, if careers depend on people being in a professional path over time, then being taken out of that path prematurely certainly disrupts someone's career. Of course, if the person can move to another firm with the same type of job with a reasonable salary, then he or she can continue his or her career, but often this is not what happens. A worker may leave his or her career in one organization but find that he or she is not able to find a job in a similar position without taking a significant pay cut and starting back at a much lower level. Occasionally, a worker may have to leave one organization and then may go back to school for a new career path or start something else that he or she might be qualified for. In either of these cases, the worker is probably going to reenter the workforce at a lower level and at a much lower salary.

When older workers are forced to leave their career before they are ready to, they often do not want to stop working and perhaps cannot afford to stop. Certainly, pensions today are not what they were for the past couple of generations of workers, and many new retirees are finding that even with a pension and Social Security, they cannot afford a reasonable (not extravagant) lifestyle without working to supplement their retirement. Therefore, you will see many older retirement-age workers in part-time jobs in retail, grocery stores, fast-food restaurants, and the like. Since they are retired, they are probably on Medicare for their health insurance, so they can work without needing health or retirement benefits, which means that by hiring people part-time, the companies are saving the money they would have to spend if they were hiring younger people full-time who needed benefits.

Careers today are very different than they used to be, and this is even true of many of the professions. It is common for doctors, lawyers, dentists, and so forth to change careers before they are ready to retire, and this is happening with greater frequency in recent years. People in the professions might work for larger organizations and thus might be in positions where younger and less expensive employees would replace them. However, even if they work for themselves in a private practice, it is getting so much more difficult to make a decent living as a professional working in an independent practice (in almost every profession) that many will leave and do something different as they get older.

Whether we feel that it is a good thing or a bad thing that jobs and careers are very different than they used to be, there have been many significant changes. Although it is likely that these changes will continue and perhaps even increase, it is important that as younger people enter the workforce, they have a clear understanding of what work is like today and that their expectations are clear and realistic. Having a plan and a course of action is very important, but having options, being well and broadly trained, being flexible and adaptable, and having backup plans are more important today than ever before.

Are Happy Workers More Productive?

It has been said for many years that "happy workers are productive workers," and although this seems logical, it turns out it is not really that simple. When we talk about the attitudes and feelings that a worker has about his or her job, this is referred to as "job satisfaction"; that is, how satisfied or dissatisfied a person is about his or her job. However, when describing the job satisfaction of a group of workers, we usually refer to this as "morale." It does makes sense that if someone likes his or her job, he or she is more likely to work harder and try to do better, so it may not be clear as to why this is not exactly true.

When we look at the relationship between job satisfaction and work performance, we find a weak positive correlation (correlation is the statistical relationship between two or more variables). What this means is that there is a relationship between job satisfaction and performance and as a positive relationship that means that as one variable increases, the other tends to increase as well; thus, the higher the job satisfaction, the higher the performance, and vice versa, the higher the performance, the higher the job satisfaction—it works both ways. However, since this is a "weak" relationship, it means that does not always hold for all workers, and in some cases, the opposite might be true. What this usually means is that there are other factors that influence both variables as well.

We can certainly see how even though we tend to like jobs better if we are good at them, it is obvious that there would be many other factors that would influence how much we like our job—for example, having good coworkers, having a good supervisor, and having good pay and benefits. Similarly, there would be other variables that would influence worker performance—for example, education and training, experience on the job, good supervision, and collaborating coworkers. Consequently, when looking at the relationship between job satisfaction and performance, the best way to summarize the research evidence is to say that "with all other factors held constant, then job satisfaction is a good predictor of performance." Of course, since all the other factors are never held constant in real life, the actual relationship between these variables is a weak positive correlation.

Another measure of worker behavior that we are usually concerned with is attendance. Once again, the relationship between attendance and job satisfaction is a weak positive correlation and for much of the same reason as to why this type of relationship is found between job satisfaction and performance. Of course, people are more likely to want to come to work on a job they really like, but it turns out that there are many other factors that determine attendance as well. For example, research evidence reports that the things that often influence worker attendance include the presence of children at home, being a single parent, not having transportation, the availability of public transportation, one's health, distance from work, and weather. You may even think of some other things that might affect worker attendance, but it is very clear that more is involved than just job satisfaction. Similarly, we can again state that all other things being held constant, the higher the job satisfaction, the greater the likelihood that a person will attend work.

One of the other work outcome variables that has been studied relative to worker job satisfaction is voluntary turnover; this refers to workers leaving a job for their own reasons—they are not laid off, retired, or fired. This relationship is a little clearer because the research finds a strong, negative relationship between job satisfaction and voluntary turnover; that is, the more a person is satisfied with his or her job, the less likely he or she is to voluntarily leave it. Of course, that does not mean that a person would never leave a job he or she likes; for example, if a worker really likes his or her job, but someone offers him or her a similar job in a good company that doubles his or her salary, has better benefits, and requires fewer hours of work, he or she would leave and take the new job. However, in general, the more satisfied a person is with his or her job, the less likely he or she is to leave it.

In summary, having happy workers is a good thing for many reasons. First, if other factors are taken care of, then they are likely to try to do a better job and are more likely to have good attendance records, although these relationships are a little more complicated, and it is not always easy to see how this works. However, it does seem to be true that the more someone likes his or her job, the less likely he or she is to leave it, and that does make good sense—especially since turnover is so expensive for companies.

Social Interaction at Work

For most people who work outside the home, their work group is one of the more important social groups that they are involved with. It is frequently true that not counting time sleeping, most people spend more time with work colleagues than with any other family member or friends. It is also true that many people have friends whom they work with and spend time socializing outside of work. Thus, when we consider "social reference groups," the work group is both social and an important group that we refer to as being important in our lives.

One thing that recent changes in jobs and careers have done, however, is to modify how we relate to and interact with work groups. As mentioned earlier, people today tend to change jobs more frequently and even change careers more than they did in the past. What that means is that the group of people we work with is often changing, and therefore, the group dynamics change, and some of the people we were close to leave their jobs, and we may not see much of them anymore. Thus, we may not get as close to people at work because they (or we) may not be around that long. Certainly, job security and career stability are not what they were in the past, and many workers do not let themselves get as close to work colleagues as they did in the past because about the time we become good friends, they may leave or we might as well. In fact, many workers today will specifically report that because job security is so uncertain in many organizations, it is not worth to get close to people knowing that the work relationship might end at any time.

Although there are changes in work relationships today, these are still important relationships for all working people, and the quality of those relationships has a lot to do with how one feels about his or her job and organization. Further, it is not only the work colleagues who are affected by layoffs, retirements, firing, or turnover, but managers are affected too. Thus, workers can never be sure that the manager or supervisor they have will be there for a while, because they may have to leave or be promoted to another position as well.

Workplace Stress, Bullying, and Burnout

It is unlikely that the workplace has ever been stress-free, but it certainly seems that work today is more fraught with stress than in times past. Although stress has always been a part of human life, including work life, the nature and types of stress today may be different for many reasons. Interestingly, stress is usually considered to be one of the negatives at work, but it is also true that too little stress is a problem too—this leads to boredom and lack of interest and commitment to the job. Thus, we want people to be interested and excited about their jobs, but we do not want them to be so "stressed out" that it interferes with their effectiveness and enjoyment of work. There are many reasons why work today produces high levels of stress for workers, and although there may be many other reasons, these are some that are very important:

> **Changes:** Any change, including good change, creates stress; the workplace today involves many changes in most jobs and companies. Changes in technology, work expectations, coworkers, supervisors, the nature of the job, competition, and globalization—probably more things change than stay the same, and change is always stressful.

> **Feelings of Helplessness/Powerlessness:** Many workers today feel that they have little control over their job or what is demanded/expected of them. Feeling helpless is bad enough, but when workers also feel powerless to make any reasonable changes, the helplessness soon becomes hopelessness. There is considerable research evidence that feelings of helplessness and hopelessness are not only related to feeling stressed but also can lead to depression.

> **The Job Itself:** Very frequently, workers complain that their job itself is very stressful. This can be due to workers being expected to do more than they can reasonably do as well as due to unclear expectations and not really knowing what one is to do. Another frequent complaint is that some workers feel that they are being asked to do things that are not really their job and may even be asked to do things they feel may be unethical or inappropriate. However, if they are being asked to do these things by their boss or manager, it is hard to know whom to complain to. Job activities that involve stressful situations like dealing with dissatisfied customers or doing dangerous tasks can also be stressful. Also, the work conditions like temperature, crowding, noise, pollution, and the like can produce and increase work stress.

> **Lack of Helpful Feedback:** Helpful feedback is information given to a person that will enable him or her to improve his or her performance. Positive

feedback like "Good job" may sound positive but is so vague that it may not help the person know what he or she is doing right or how he or she can improve. Similarly, negative feedback like "You are just a loser" is also not helpful. Good positive feedback tells a person exactly what he or she did that was correct and usually involves helpful comments that make the person want to continue to do a good job. Helpful negative feedback tells a person what he or she has done that was not up to expectation and what he or she needs to do to improve his or her performance. This helpful negative feedback can then become a goal for future improvement. The lack of helpful feedback creates uncertainly in workers that can certainly become a source of stress.

Lack of Good Person-Job or Person-Organization Fit: It makes good sense that people should do a better job and be happier if they are well suited for their position at work. It is referred to as person-job fit when we describe how a worker "fits" with his or her job. In the past, it was clear that good person-job fit was a good predictor of job satisfaction and job performance. In recent years, we find that it is not as good a predictor as it was in the past. This is understandable since jobs change frequently, and thus, a person may have more trouble being comfortable with his or her position. Further, people change jobs and organizations more frequently than they did in the past, and this too will keep a person from feeling as connected and committed to his or her job.

In fact, recent evidence suggests that person-organization fit is more important in determining how successful and happy a worker will be today. Since jobs tend to change frequently, even in the same organization, how well a person identifies with the organization will be more important than how he or she relates to his or her specific job. However, since workers are also changing organizations more frequently than in the past, it is true that they may not feel as closely connected to their organization either, which means that we will probably find that over time, the worker-organization fit may not be as good a predictor as it has been in recent years.

Traumatic Events at Work: Whenever a person experiences significant traumatic events in their lives, it will produce stress, and this is certainly true of such events in the workplace. The obvious example would involve things like crime or workplace violence. Some jobs like being a police officer, firefighter, or combat military personnel are certainly likely candidates for traumatic events at work. This is clear why these professions are very susceptible to posttraumatic stress disorder, and this is a very serious problem for all of them. However, trauma can occur in any workplace, and criminal activities like robbery, assault, and violence may be brought into the workplace by people from outside the organization, but problems can also originate within the organization itself.

Nonviolent Aggression at Work: As frightening and tragic as workplace violence can be, it is still not something that happens frequently. Since our nightly news takes us all over the country and around the world, we are exposed to more of these violent events than in the past, but even one of these tragedies is one too many, and most organizations are doing a much better job of security and protection of employees and customers. Sometimes we get annoyed with some of the security measures, but the intention is clearly to make the workplace safer for everyone.

A much more common problem in organizations is nonviolent aggression like bullying and other forms of abuse. This has become a more frequent type of problem and has gotten even worse because of the frequent abuse of social media by some people. This type of stress is not as obvious and rarely reported but is extremely stressful and leads to many difficulties in the workplace, including decreased productivity and job satisfaction.

The Costs of Job Stress

According to a report published by the University of Massachusetts at Lowell, job stress is estimated to cost American businesses over $300 billion per year. The very substantial amount of money is due to stress-related health care costs, disability expenses, absenteeism, decreased productivity, and voluntary job turnover; further, research demonstrates that 40 percent of voluntary job turnover is due to stress. Other findings about the costs of stress in the workplace include:

- Health care costs are 50 percent higher for employees who report high levels of stress.
- Job stress is the cause of more health complaints than financial or family problems.
- Replacing an employee costs 120–200 percent of the salary for the position affected.
- The average cost for absenteeism in a large company is almost $4 million per year.
- Depression is the largest single predictor of absenteeism and work-related performance problems, and work stress is one of the risk factors for depression; depression in employees is associated with 10 sick days taken per year.
- For every 45 cents spent on treating depression, further 53 cents are spent indirectly on absenteeism, presenteeism (where a worker is present but not working up to his or her full capacity), and disability.
- Information from the insurance industry reports that insurance claims for stress-related industrial accidents costs about twice as much as nonstress-related accidents.

Clearly, stress is a major cost factor for all businesses and organizations, and finding ways to minimize the negative impact of stress is not only good for employees but also good for business. Some companies almost pride themselves as to how much stress their organization produces and then will say things like, "This is a tough business; anyone not tough enough to take it, should leave." While that sounds almost reasonable to some people, the reality is that when an organization has very high stress, this will lead to higher voluntary turnover, and although many managers would expect that the "deadwood" would leave, that is often not the case. Very frequently, in high-stress work environments, the first people to leave are the talented workers who are good enough to get a better job in a different company quickly. Thus, the business ends up losing employees they would rather keep and keeping the ones they would rather lose.

The Employers' Responsibility to Reduce Workplace Stress

Some people feel that employee stress is their problem, and it is not the responsibility of the organization to deal with worker stress. However, since we have established that stress is very costly for a business, it seems that controlling or reducing stress would be one way that managers could help a company be more financially sound. One study found that for every dollar that employers spent on programs to reduce stress, and to help workers have better physical and mental health, saved the company $5; that seems like a good investment from a financial standpoint. It is also true that the employer has control of many of the things that might be producing stress. For example, unrealistic time demands, unrealistic expectations for the work a person must do, asking workers to perform tasks clearly outside of their area of expertise or responsibility in addition to the other regular things that they must do for their own job are things that employers have some control over. Further, insuring that people are paid fairly and have reasonable benefits is very important for managing stress. For example, if a company does not have paid sick leave, then employees who are ill may come to work so they do not lose pay but then infect other workers who will either have to leave work or will not perform as well. In a similar vein, if a company does not provide health insurance, then not only will people be likely to come to work sick, but they may also not be able to afford to go to the doctor to take care of their medical problems.

In most countries, and certainly in the United States, companies have legal responsibilities to provide safe and healthy workplaces. While many businesses find these requirements a nuisance, requiring safer work environments has saved thousands of lives and has also saved millions of dollars in accidents that have been prevented. Thus, providing a safe and healthy work environment is one of the positive things that organizations can do to improve the quality of people's work lives.

Another example of legal responsibility for companies is preventing sexual harassment. As the percentage of women workers has increased in recent years, there has been a significant increase in the frequency of sexual harassment complaints. When a worker is being sexually harassed, this obviously produces stress and will also affect job satisfaction, productivity, and attendance; it will also affect turnover. Companies who try to provide an environment where sexual harassment is not accepted or tolerated will find that this has many benefits to the employees and to the organization itself.

Issues of prejudice and discrimination are also significant causes of workplace stress and are things that also involve legal and statutory protection. Organizations that do not protect workers from discrimination and prejudice are in violation of civil rights and other regulations and laws. These kinds of violations cost companies millions of dollars every year in lawsuits and fines, and these costs are 100 percent preventable just by providing a workplace where these kinds of practices and attitudes are not tolerated.

Many employers do not realize that a considerable amount of stress produced in the workplace because of psychological and social factors can be managed. One of the main sources of stress that workers complain about is supervisory and/or managerial styles. It has been demonstrated that when managers are well trained and rewarded for being effective in their jobs, they have more positive and productive management styles. Too often, managers are so focused on short-term financial goals that they lose sight of the longer term and often more important goals. You can only tell people so many times that they "have to do more with less," and what this usually means is that they may lay off people to save money and then expect the remaining workers to do the same amount of work or more, but with fewer people. This strategy only works if all the workers were intentionally underproducing to begin with. Some managers expect that most workers are loafers, and by yelling at them and demanding higher productivity, the workers will simply do what they are told. Certainly, one of the best ways to reduce stress at work is to train and support supervisors and managers to manage effectively and responsibly and to give them reasonable and attainable goals as well.

It is common for organizations to try to cut costs by decreasing the workforce, but this is sometimes a very risky strategy. For example, nurses in many hospitals complain about being short-staffed and not having enough nurses to adequately meet patient needs. Because of the nature of what they do, their contracts often allow for mandatory overtime when needed and even be required to work "mandatory doubles" where a nurse will work two shifts in a row. Not only is this a questionable practice if it happens more than rarely, but it is dangerous too. Research has demonstrated that nursing mistakes and medication errors happen most frequently when nurses work more than a regular eight-hour shift. If we give any value to the lives and health of the patients (which is what all hospitals ought to do), and we want to avoid malpractice, wrongful death, and liability lawsuits, it seems that having adequate staffing should be something that would be normal; unfortunately, in many hospitals that is not the case. Very recently, I heard two different nurses report to me that they resigned from their nursing position at a local hospital because they felt that they were risking their license every time they came to work. Another physician colleague of mine recommended that when one of my family members went into the hospital, we should try to have someone stay with the patient most of the time because the nursing coverage was not adequate to meet all the patient needs and a family person should be there to make sure that everything was being done that was needed.

Another thing that many organizations are doing is to provide employees more flexibility in determining their schedules. For example, flextime is where a person works the normal number of hours but he or she can determine how he or she splits the hours up. There will usually be guidelines like you must work eight hours, and it can be in one or two segments neither of which would be less than two hours; you can work any eight hours in one or two sessions any time between 4 a.m. and 10.p.m., but you must overlap at least two hours every day with your supervisor; and, you must keep the same schedule for at least a month before you can modify it. Flextime dramatically reduces worker stress because it minimizes the work-home conflicts and allows people to meet their work and other needs as effectively as possible. Research has indicated that in most cases, flextime results in increased productivity as well.

In addition to flextime, some organizations will allow telecommuting, which means that people can work on their computer from home at least part of the time and still get the work done that needs to be done. While there are some downsides to working from home (e.g., decreased contact with colleagues and supervisors), most employees find that this not only reduces stress but helps them be more productive as well.

Some of the other things that employers can do to reduce stress at work include using job satisfaction surveys of employees and looking at the data to see what kinds of things are creating problems for the workers and then paying attention to the issues and try to make the situations better.

Some organizations do a very good job of reducing worker stress by trying to make the workplace more supportive and healthier. Having programs for such things as stopping smoking, losing weight, preparing for retirement, and many others have proven to be effective and helpful. Some organizations provide a gym, outdoor hiking trails, and other opportunities for exercise that are very effective in reducing stress. Others will provide things like day care programs, English as a second language courses, career counseling, financial/budgeting advice, and many others. One very productive software development company, SAS, in North Carolina has in-house day care, maternity and paternity leave, leave for adoptive parents, in-house barber and beauty shops, and a service where people can bring their dry cleaning with them to work where it is picked up and then returned a few days later. Some companies feel that they cannot afford such programs, but if you look at research that demonstrates that these positive types of programs lead to reduced turnover, hiring of better candidates, decreased absenteeism, improved job satisfaction, and higher productivity, these costs become insignificant. Further, some companies have found that they might need to charge small fees for some of these services and not only do employees pay for them, but they are usually glad to do so.

SUGGESTIONS FOR IMPROVING THE POSITIVES AND MINIMIZING THE NEGATIVES AT WORK

It is clear there are many complicating factors that make work much different than it has been in the past. Jobs and careers are different, the workforce is different, competition is different, the nature of work is different, and work life is and will continue to be very stressful. The job of every organization and every employee is to try to take advantage of the positive things that this new work environment provides and try to reduce and minimize some of the negative and difficult problems in the workplace today. This may sound unrealistically optimistic, but it is essential if we are to be as effective and productive as possible—for both workers and organizations. There are some very realistic and important things that organizations, managers/supervisors, and employees can do to take advantage of what we know to make the workplace more positive for everyone.

One thing that managers and supervisors can do that will make a big difference in the workplace is to *listen*. In most organizations, managers and supervisors spend most of their time telling people what to do. However, employees, now more than ever, expect to be listened to and considered. Employees today are also ambitious and well educated and often have good ideas. Further, if you want to motivate an employee, listen to what is important to him or her, and you should have some good ideas as to what will make the employee want to work harder. Managers sometime feel that what all employees seem to do is to complain and do not ever have anything positive to add. Of course, this is not true, but it might feel like this is the way things are to the manager. If employees are given a chance to speak up about things and they feel like they are being heard, they will also be more inclined to offer helpful suggestions and not just complain about negative things. However, when employees do complain or have negative comments, they should make sure that they are talking about an issue about which something can be done; they could even try to make suggestions as to how things could be changed for the better. Even when their suggestions are not followed, when employees feel that they have been listened to and their ideas at least fairly considered, this does make a difference in how they feel and how motivated they will be to try to do a better job.

Another thing that many organizations do not do but can make a difference by adding positive elements to a person's work is to give him or her more autonomy over how he or she does his or her job. Usually, employees know more about their job than their managers do, but they often have little control over how they do their job and may even be required to do things in ways that make their job more difficult and might interfere with their productivity and job satisfaction. Managers should be concerned about *what* gets done rather than how it's done—assuming, of course, that what is being done is safe, ethical, and appropriate. However, many managers and supervisors spent considerable time "micromanaging" employees and watching and interfering with how the jobs are being done and therefore actually interfering with job effectiveness. Of course, if a person is not producing up to expectations, then it is the manager's responsibility to try to determine the cause of the decreased productivity and to help the employee find ways to improve his or her performance. However, many managers have found that by giving employees more authority in their jobs, they not only appreciate the opportunities, but they do a better job as well.

One factor that will certainly improve the "positives" in the workplace is to provide people with challenging and important work that is recognized and rewarded. Many managers feel that a person should just accept that they must do their job, and therefore it has to be important. Workers should be shown how their job relates to the performance and outcomes of the whole organization and why their work does make a difference. Recognizing good performance does include getting adequate pay and benefits and getting raises when it is appropriate, but recognition should also involve much more than just the monetary factors; there is a lot of value in a sincere "Thanks for doing such a good job." Similarly, workers will do a better job and feel good about it if they are given timely and meaningful feedback. Annual performance reviews are important, but even more important is feedback on a continuing basis to let people know what they are doing well and what might need to be improved. Providing helpful feedback makes a huge difference to worker satisfaction and performance. Even if the feedback is "constructive" and is meant to show someone what he or she is doing wrong, this feedback can now become a goal for improvement, and when the person starts doing a better job, this can be recognized and rewarded.

Setting meaningful and important goals is also something that will help improve the quality of the workplace for employees and managers. A good manager does not just assign goals but also helps employees set goals that are important for them individually as well as important for the organization to meet its objectives. To be most effective and to have the best results, goal setting should be collaborative—managers and employees should set goals together that optimize individual *and* organizational performance.

Many organizations today are working with "team-based" management, and this may often not be done as effectively as possible. Too often, managers believe that team management just means telling employees what to do in groups rather than individually. Of course, team-based management means much more than this and involves shared authority and responsibility and requires more communication and meetings. Most employees will say that meetings are usually time-wasters that keep them away from doing their jobs. However, organizations depend upon meetings to be able to function effectively. The problem is not just having meetings but having unnecessary or poorly run meetings as well. If an organization wants meetings to be effective, then they need to train managers and employees as to how to work more effectively in teams and how to get the most out of meetings. In a team-based organization, time must be provided for collaborative work opportunities, including meetings, but they also must have space that is appropriate for group and team meetings. Further, it is important for organizations to have space available for normal social interactions at work—break rooms, lunch rooms, and the like can be very helpful. Some organizations feel that these kinds of spaces just lead to loafing and avoiding work. Research has found that these kinds of social spaces lead to people talking more about work than other things and that social settings improve the quality of organizational communication. It is also true that, since the work group is an important social reference group for most people, having more opportunities to interact socially with one's coworkers is a distinctly positive element in most workplaces and will improve both the quality of work and job performance.

Finally, most organizations can do a much better job of is training. Among the major industrialized countries in the world, the United States is very low on the scale of money spent by organizations for training. As technologies change, there must be training to help people deal with the new requirements, but even the training for new employees to simply learn about the organization, what it does, and how it works is very important and usually results in new employees becoming more productive sooner. Training is one opportunity for management to help employees find ways to minimize some of the negative factors in the workplace and improve on the positives. Companies that feel that they do not have the time or money for more training are missing an opportunity to be more effective and more profitable/productive in the future.

SUMMARY AND CONCLUSION

We will never find ways to eliminate all the negative factors associated with work. It will always take time and energy, even if it gets easier in the future. Too often we simply expect that work is negative and there is nothing we can do about it. However, that is rarely the case; both workers and managers have an investment in the workplace being more positive, and by working together, there is an opportunity to reduce the negatives and enhance the positives. People should go to work with the idea that they can and will do a good job, and that when they are done with a day's work, they can feel good about what they have done. This is something that we can all work toward in our own lives and in our own jobs—doing a better job and enjoying it more.

4

Who: Psychologists' Theories about Work

Psychologists have many theories about human beings, and each of them looks at people a little differently. Although most theorists do not have extensive theories about work itself, most of the theories of human personality either directly address issues of work or at least imply how work fits into a person's life. As we explore these various theories about people and work, it may be tempting to try to decide which of these theories is actually "right." Many books and articles have been written explaining, agreeing with, challenging, or criticizing each of the theories we will address, but there are some things that would be helpful to remember as you read about each of these theories.

First, none of them are completely correct and all of them have elements that either have not or cannot be proven and even things that have not been supported by research. Second, each of them has some points that are supportable and verifiable, and thus there are parts of each theory that appear to be correct and important. You should look at these theories from the standpoint of what does each of them tell you that helps you understand human personality and how work fits in as part of the human condition. When you have completed reading this book, you will probably have your own theory about personality and work, and the value of that is that you will now have a way to understand people and work more effectively and will have a way of organizing facts and information about human personality and work. Even if your theory is not "right" or cannot be proven with research, it is still something that you may find helpful and interesting.

We are going to address certain types of theories generally and give you some examples of each type of theory and how they either address or imply how work would fit into their views. Some theories look inside the person's mind and what is going on inside, some will address overt behavior and how people learn and respond, other address how people think and perceive, and some look at people as unique and special and try to address their humanity and free will as fundamental issues in the human condition.

PSYCHODYNAMIC THEORIES

The psychodynamic theories are ones that believe that the important aspects of human psychology are inside of the person's "psyche." That means they feel that most of the important parts of a person's psychology are inside their mind (psyche), and how these factors interact will produce thoughts feelings and behaviors. There are several types of psychodynamic theories; we will explore how they differ and how they conceive of and deal with the psychology of work.

Sigmund Freud

The first and most important psychodynamic theory was Freud's psychoanalysis. Freud started working on this theory in the late 1800s and continued to work on the theory and treat patients until his death in 1939. He was born in Austria and lived most of his life in Vienna, but when the Nazis came into power and started persecuting Jews (Freud was Jewish), he took his family and moved to London, England, where he lived until his death. In Austria, he went to medical school and became a physician; he was very interested in neurophysiological research and did some very important work. However, he also found that he could not make a living just doing research, so he decided to become a consulting neurologist and started working with Josef Breuer treating patients with hysteria (a mental condition characterized by anxiety and physical symptoms). He later went to Paris to study ways of treating hysteria, and with this new knowledge and the influence of the French doctors and researchers he was working with, he started developing his own theory and treatment methods.

Freudian psychoanalysis is a theory of personality, a theory of psychopathology (abnormal psychology), and a method of treatment. Freud was a brilliant and captivating teacher and started attracting many very bright and interesting professionals who want to learn from him. Although he was very well known as a doctor, there were few psychologists or psychiatrists who would even try to treat the things that Freud was dealing with, and thus, many people became his patients. In fact, people would come to him from all over the world and stay in Vienna from months or even years to complete their treatment with Freud. In addition, many young professionals came to Vienna to study with Freud and to learn about psychoanalysis. However, as popular as he was with many people, the traditional medical societies were very disturbed with the unorthodox and disturbing ideas in Freud's theory, and he was largely ostracized from the traditional medical community until later in his life.

Freud thought that the mind was made up of three "layers": the conscious, which involved the things that you were thinking about; the preconscious, which included things that you might not be thinking about but could immediately bring to mind if you directed your attention to them—for example, "what did you have for breakfast?"; and the subconscious (or unconscious), which contained all of the basic sexual and aggressive instincts that all people have and also contained the painful and troubling memories that were too difficult to experience in the conscious mind and were therefore filed away in the subconscious where they would not trouble us (at least consciously).

In addition to the "levels of consciousness," Freud also postulated three different "organs" of personality: The id, the ego, and the superego. These are terms that you may have heard of but probably mean something different than you might think. According to Freud, the id is the basic part of the personality that we are born with. It is comprised of our basic sexual and aggressive instincts and it is all in the subconscious—we never experience elements of the id directly in consciousness. The id is always pressing for immediate gratification of all of its needs, which is obviously impossible, but that does not change anything because the id is not rational and only deals with basic instincts. Since the id's needs can never be met immediately in entirety, as the infant starts encountering reality, another organ of personality begins to emerge: the ego. This part of personality is found in all levels of the personality: conscious, preconscious, and subconscious. The ego is the adaptive organ of personality that continues to learn ways of meeting at least some of the Id's needs in a reasonable amount of time and with respect to reality and our conscience, which is part of the last part of personality to emerge: the superego. As we begin learning the "rules" of society, the values that our parents and families teach us, we begin to adopt and live by these guidelines, and the superego begins to form and becomes our conscience and sets a standard (the Superego Ideal) that we try to live up to.

Freud also postulated a sequence of psychosexual developmental stages that all people go through, and how well we go through the stages and deal with the relevant conflicts in each stage will determine how healthy we are as adult human beings. When we encounter difficulties in our development, we may start to develop anxiety, which is very unpleasant and something that we try to avoid or control. According to Freud, we use "psychological defenses" to protect ourselves from anxiety, and these include such things as denial (we act as if there is no conflict or problem) and repression, which is where we take unpleasant events, instincts, thoughts or feelings, or traumatic things and push them down into the subconscious so we do not have to think about them at all. Of course, when we rely too heavily on psychological defenses, this produces difficulties that are manifest as psychological disorders, but all people do use defenses, and used normally, they help us adapt and survive and that helps us be "normal." Defenses are only a problem if they are overused or clearly dysfunctional.

Psychoanalytic theory primarily addresses abnormal behavior and its treatment, but he did talk about "normal" behavior and even had some things to say about work. Of course, for Freud, all behavior is derived from the sexual and aggressive instincts that underlie all our thoughts, feelings, and actions. Therefore, work is about satisfying our basic needs and therefore is about survival of the individual and the society. Once Freud was asked what he thought "normal" behavior involved, his answer was "Lieben und Arbeiten": to love and to work. So he felt that a healthy person would be able to love others and have rewarding love relationships and to carry on the basic tasks of life—to work. He also theorized about a psychological defense called "sublimation," and this refers to an adaptive strategy whereby a person cannot express or even acknowledge frightening and anxiety-provoking instincts like the sexual and aggressive impulses in the id, and therefore, we modify those instincts into socially acceptable motives and activities like work. Thus, by working we are then able to reduce some of the anxiety from these subconscious instincts, help ourselves survive and prosper, and benefit society. Clearly, Freud believed that work was necessary for survival of the individual and society.

When it came to Freud's theory, he was a very jealous parent and did not welcome criticism or modification of his ideas by others. He did clarify and improve his theory over his life, but he did not like the "tampering" by others. As you might expect, this led to some conflict with a few of his followers who were intelligent and ambitious and had their own ideas about human psychology and did not always agree with Freud.

Alfred Adler

Adler was a very bright and ambitious young man who was one of Freud's early followers but who started having some questions and disagreements with Freud about some of the foundations of psychoanalysis. Adler did not believe that human psychology was only based on sexual and aggressive instincts, and he thought that in addition to people having healthy and positive drives and instincts, they were basically social beings who needed and wanted rewarding relationships with others. He also focused on many important and popular issues of the day, including such things as equality, parent education, birth order, lifestyle, and the holism of individuals. In this sense, "holism" refers to the idea that people are not made up of different parts of the personality (e.g., id, ego, and superego) that were continually in conflict with one another. Rather, he argued that human psychology has a unifying inner force that integrates the different elements of our personality into one coherent whole. Things like "style of life" and patterns of coping were essential for us to understand people better, according to Adler.

Adler's ideas were very popular, and he found an enthusiastic audience in the United States where he was a frequent guest and speaker. Rather than the strict intrapsychic determinism of Freud who felt that all behavior was caused by internal (primarily subconscious) factors, Adler believed that people have unique and individual goals and that these goals could be reached by people creatively using their own "self-determination," a term that Freud had little use for.

For Adler, mental health was found in a feeling of human connectedness and a willingness to develop oneself fully and contribute to the welfare of others. The importance of people feeling a part of a community was one of the foundations of what he thought it meant to be human. Even his treatment tended to focus on social and relationship issues and addressed mostly contemporary issues rather than the early childhood that psychoanalysts focused on. In terms of work, Adler expected that people would work to improve themselves, contributing to the community as well as their own family.

Adler was the first of the early Freudians to break away the idea of sexual and aggressive instincts in favor of social and self-fulfillment needs. He and Freud did not like one another's theory, nor did they have much affection or respect for one another. However, Adler's ideas affected many other emerging theorists and practitioners, and many who followed learned from his ideas of self-determination, social causation, humanism (the inherent value of the human being), and relationships. There are still practitioners today who very closely follow Adler's ideas and approaches.

Carl Jung

Jung was a Swiss psychiatrist who became interested in Freudian psycho-analysis because he shared an interest in the unconscious and its role in human psychology. He was very bright and had some new and different ways of examining human psychology. Freud and Jung became very close and corresponded frequently. In fact, when Freud was invited to lecture in the United States, Jung was invited to come with him. However, in one of his lectures, he criticized Freud's idea regarding the sexual nature of human drives and instincts, and this led to a split between the two that was never repaired, and they never spoke or communicated again.

Jung looks at the unconscious a little differently than Freud. He did believe that the human psyche was made up of different and interacting systems, including the ego, the personal unconscious, and the collective unconscious. The ego, much like psychoanalysis, is the adaptive organ of personality and helps the person deal with the interaction of the other ele-ments of the psyche and with external reality. The personal unconscious is very much like Freud's idea of the unconscious and is the repository of things that have been forgotten or were so traumatic and upsetting that they were submerged in the unconscious so that they did not bother the person's conscious life. The one thing that sets Jung's theory apart from Freud's and most other theories as well is the idea of the collective uncon-scious. This is an original and very controversial aspect of his theory. He sees this as a repository of latent memories from our ancestral and evo-lutionary past and is shared with all members of our species. Thus, things like fears of the dark, fear of snakes and bugs, desires to take care of chil-dren, and so forth are based on evolutionary experiences that have survival benefits and are therefore "stamped" on the human ancestral mind and become part of the genetic endowment of all people.

Part of the collective unconscious involves "archetypes," which are images and thoughts that have universal meanings that may be manifest in dreams, literature, myths, art, and religions. By studying philosophy, anthropology, comparative religion, archeology, and art, Jung made a case for the universal symbolism of certain themes and ideas. One of these archetypes is the "self," which provides a sense of unity in our experiences. Jung would have seen work as an activity that would be consistent with the self because it would help unify and support our lives, families, and social groups. In addition, since work also has significant survival value, it would be seen as part of the collective unconscious and brought forward through evolution as something that we all share in various different degrees.

As interesting as Jung's ideas are, his theory was never as well accepted as Freud's or others of that era. However, there are even people today who still value and utilize Jungian theory and therapy. His contributions are noteworthy but more from a historical perspective than anything else. Because he did not specifically write with the general public in mind, most of his writings are cumbersome to read and difficult to understand.

Karen Horney

Some of the newer psychoanalysts followed Adler in focusing on social factors rather than on the sexual and aggressive instincts that Freud relied on. Karen Horney was trained in Europe with the classical psychoanalytic model although she had some concerns about Freud's theory. Unlike Freud, she felt that social and cultural conditions, and particularly childhood experiences, are responsible for shaping the personality. Of course, Freud did recognize the importance of childhood experiences, but he emphasized how these experiences influenced the underlying unconscious forces that directed the human psyche. She also felt that Freud did not treat female psychology appropriately, and she did address some of her concerns by expanding the rather unexplored area of the psychology of women. She also was very influential in developing a more modern approach to psychotherapy and was recognized as one of the leading teachers in the training of new analysts. In fact, after moving to the United States, she was one of the founders of the Chicago Psychoanalytic Institute, which is still in place today.

With respect to work, Horney saw work as a normal and healthy activity that people who were not neurotic (psychologically troubled) would approach as a way of becoming autonomous and self-fulfilled. This would enable them to have a positive approach to life and relationships and allow them to support themselves and their families in a way that would lead to a lifestyle that would result in a full and rewarding life. One thing that she would have focused on in her approach to work that was different from other theorists of the time was the emphasis on the place of the psychology of women. She saw the importance of women having a sense that the work that they chose was something that was based on their needs and goals and not just the enactment of the social and cultural roles that defined the "work" of women as wives, mothers, and caretakers; these roles were important to Horney, but she insisted that women should have access to other roles that were not just based on the expectations of others.

Erik Erikson

Erikson is another example of a more socially oriented psychoanalyst who, unlike many of the other analysts, was not medically trained although he was college educated. Having grown up in Germany, he had also traveled extensively and came to Vienna where he was exposed to psychoanalysis when he came to teach art at the school that was set up for the children of patients who were being treated by Freud. He became interested in psychoanalysis and was largely trained by Anna Freud (Sigmund's daughter). He later moved to the United States where he taught at the University of California at Berkeley and later at Harvard University.

Erikson always claimed that his theory was not in contrast to Freudian psychoanalysis but described processes that ran parallel to Freud's theory of development, and his theory was primarily about "psychosocial development." He was also very clear in emphasizing that his theory was not a collection of facts, but rather a structure that enabled one to think about human psychology in an orderly and logical fashion. His theory focused on these psychosocial stages each of which had a primary "crisis" that needed to be dealt with and a basic virtue that would result if the crisis was suitably dealt with. His psychosocial stage theory is summarized in Table 4.1.

As you can see, this theory addresses many of the issues that most people address during their life development, and because it is so easy to understand and relate to, this theory has been widely accepted as a good model for social development. It must also be noted that this theory was not based on empirical research, but then neither were any of the other psychodynamic theories, which is one of the main criticisms of this type of theory. However, Erikson never claimed that his

Table 4.1. Erikson's Psychosocial Stages of Development

Psychosocial Crisis	Basic Virtue	Age
Trust vs. Mistrust	Hope	Infancy (0–1 ½)
Autonomy vs. Shame	Will	Early Childhood (1 ½–3)
Initiative vs. Guilt	Purpose	Play Age (3–5)
Industry vs. Inferiority	Competency	School Age (5–12)
Ego Identity vs. Role Confusion	Fidelity	Adolescence (12–18)
Intimacy vs. Isolation	Love	Young Adult (18–40)
Generativity vs. Stagnation	Care	Adulthood (40–65)
Ego Integrity vs. Despair	Wisdom	Maturity (65+)

theory was based on scientific facts but was largely based on observation and logic.

There are several ways to look at Erikson's theory regarding the psychology of work. Looking at each stage and the virtue associated with it, let us approach them from a psychology of work perspective:

- **Trust versus Mistrust:** Developing trust leads to hope, which allows a person to set goals and aspire to a life that enables him or her to be productive and live a healthy and rewarding life.
- **Autonomy versus Shame:** Developing a sense of autonomy leads to the emergence of will, which gives a person the sense that he or she can approach life as an independent and autonomous adult who can make decisions and choices about what is best for him or her as a life course—including work that will help him or her become the person he or she wants to be.
- **Initiative versus Guilt:** Achieving a sense of initiative leads to a person feeling that his or her life has purpose and that choosing a job consistent with his or her life's purpose is something that he or she can do with confidence.
- **Industry versus Inferiority:** As the child gets involved with school, he or she begins to see that if he or she works hard and learns the skills that he or she will need to be successful in life, he or she will develop a sense of competency, which means that the child will believe that he or she is capable of performing at acceptable levels in his or her chosen tasks (including work and jobs).
- **Ego Identity versus Role Confusion:** As the child enters adolescence, there are many changes in his or her life; his or her body changes, his or her roles change, his or her activities change, and he or she is now expected to start trying to find out "who he or she really is." Having a secure and solid sense of identity allows people to also have fidelity, which means that they can be counted on in relationships and in social positions, including work.
- **Intimacy versus Isolation:** The young adult will start making choices about how he or she will spend the next phase of his or her life. What job and/or career will he or she choose? Will he or she get married and have a family? Will he or she live alone or with others? By moving successfully through this phase of life, the person is now capable of love, which means that he or she can have rewarding and meaningful relationships in his or her life. However, this

also means that the person needs to find ways to have love be a part of his or her life and balance out the work and responsibility part of his or her life as well. This is very similar to the thinking of Freud who said that psychological health meant that the person is capable of being able to "love and to work."

- **Generativity versus Stagnation:** During adulthood, it is important that people learn to care for the things that are important to them. These things would include things like a life partner or spouse, children or other younger people, family and elders, coworkers, society and the community, and many other things as well. This is the part of a person's life where he or she is making his or her primary contributions that he or she would hope to be remembered for.
- **Ego-Integrity versus Despair:** As adults enter their elder years if they have taken care of the things that they needed to do in their earlier years, they will go into their maturity with a sense of who they are and what they have done; their life will make sense to them, and this leads to their being able to look at, appreciate, and share their experiences and all that they have learned—wisdom. This stage is the culmination of everything that a person's life was about, including work.

As you can see, Erikson's theory very nicely addresses many of the issues of the psychology of work. As psychosocial theory, this approach allows for the various different aspects of work to be included in people's development throughout their lives.

Summary of Psychodynamic Theories

As different as these theories may seem from one another, there are some very important elements that link them together. For example, they all believe (some more strongly than others) that behavior is caused by knowable elements. Some, like Adler, do talk about self-determination and free will, but most of the psychodynamic theorists are deterministic—that is, they see behavior as "caused" by something inside or outside of the person. All of these theorists focus on "psychodynamics," which refers to what happens inside of the mind of the individual. Some emphasize unconscious factors more than conscious ones, but all of them look at what happens inside the person's mind that leads to thoughts, feelings, and actions. It is also true that all of them saw the importance of childhood in determining adult personality.

While most of these theories didn't have much to say about work spe-cifically, the more socially based theories like those of Adler, Horney, and Erikson either directly or indirectly dealt with issues related to work as a human activity. The psychodynamic theories are not as widely supported today as they were some decades ago, but there are still profes-sionals and academics who would consider themselves to be psychody-namically oriented. There are few people who would disagree that part of human psychology does involve factors below or outside of our normal consciousness, and although these things might be part of who we are and why we do the things that we do, it is not widely accepted that these unconscious factors are the main factors that are responsible for deter-mining our behavior.

BEHAVIORAL THEORIES

Although Freud was developing his theory, and psychologists were strug-gling with psychology's identity, there were many different opinions as to what psychology was and should be. Many psychologists were like philoso-phers trying to make sense of how and why people do, think, and feel the things that they do; others were like Freud trying to understand the inner workings of the human mind. However, particularly in the United States, there were some, primarily academic, psychologists who were com-mitted to the "science" of psychology and did not want to study people by philosophizing or speculating about their "unconscious"; these psycholo-gists wanted to use the methods and ideas from the sciences and were com-mitted to studying human behavior through experimentation and scientific inquiry. These more scientifically oriented psychologists tended to study human functions like sensation and perception and were also interested in looking at human behavior as their primary data. Called "behaviorists," these psychologists were only interested in studying those aspects of human psychology that could be dealt with primarily by observa-tion and experimentation.

John Watson

One of the first and most influential of the behaviorists was John Watson who was a professor of psychology at Johns Hopkins University in Baltimore, Maryland. Watson was a "radical behaviorist" because he was only interested in studying overt behavior and had no interest in things like thoughts and emotions since they could not be studied directly.

He felt strongly that psychology was the "science of behavior" and that all behavior was learned—both normal and abnormal behavior. He was exposed to the research of a Russian physiologist by the name of Ivan Pavlov, who, while studying the digestive processes in dogs, discovered that his canine subjects could be "taught" to salivate in response to a bell. Many have heard of Pavlov's work, and as important as his work was for psychology, he certainly did not consider himself to be a psychologist and dismissed the idea that his work was psychological in nature because he considered most psychology to be speculative philosophy.

What Pavlov discovered, however, was that when he was studying how the presence of meat paste on the tongue of a dog caused salivation, an interesting and puzzling result arose—after having the meat paste on its tongue even one time, the dogs would begin salivating when Pavlov entered the room. This is certainly not surprising to anyone who is coming home from work or school knowing that his or her favorite dinner is being prepared at home and starting to salivate as he or she thinks about it. However, for a physiologist, this "unstimulated drooling" was hard to explain. Pavlov was truly a brilliant researcher and decided to study it further, and he discovered what is now called "classical (or Pavlovian) conditioning." This works when there is an unconditioned stimulus (e.g., meat paste) that reliably produces a given unconditioned response (e.g., salivation). If there is a neutral stimulus (called an unconditioned stimulus; e.g., a bell) that has no effect on the unconditioned response (e.g., salivating) and it is paired with the conditioned stimulus, the unconditioned response will still occur. Thus, if one puts the meat paste on the dog's tongue and rings a bell, the dog will salivate. After pairing the unconditioned and conditioned stimulus a few times (sometimes only once is enough), we have a new response that has been learned—the conditioned response, and now the conditioned stimulus (bell) alone will produce the conditioned response (salivation).

Although Pavlov was not particularly interested in the psychological implications of his work, Watson and others were quick to pick up on this model and develop an entire theory of learning based on this new concept of conditioning. Early in the 20th century, Watson demonstrated very convincingly that many different types of behavior could be conditioned using classical conditioning and even showed how abnormal behavior like a phobia (fear) could be conditioned in a young child. This study was very controversial since it involved doing experiments on youngsters and "teaching" them abnormal behavior. Fortunately, some of his graduate students later did another study on a different child who already had a phobia and showed that conditioning techniques could also be used to "cure" a child of a phobia, and this was the first example of what was later to grow into what today we call "behavior therapy."

The classical conditioning approach can also be used to understand why certain stimuli lead to effective work behavior and others lead to less desirable work habits. Certainly, this type of conditioning approach is often used in the design of training programs for workers. Thus, if we look at work behavior and skills as learned responses, then understanding how to apply conditioning techniques to the work environment with the goal of changing and improving work behavior and skills should be a very reasonable thing for managers and consultants to try to apply.

B. F. Skinner

Skinner was also very interested in the behavioral approach to psychology, and he certainly felt that psychology was the science of behavior. He did not deny the inner working of the nervous system and the brain, but he insisted that those things were the province of the biologist, and the behavioral psychologist had no need to look inside of the "black box" of the human mind—behavior was the only data that the psychologist needed to deal with. Although Skinner was very aware of Pavlov and Watson's work, he felt that there was another type of learning that was also very significant in understanding how people learn and behave. In classical conditioning, we begin with an unconditioned stimulus that evokes an unconditioned response, and then through a process of association, the learning of new responses occurs. Skinner was less concerned with the stimuli that preceded a behavior and was more interested in what happened after the response. Building on the earlier work of Edwin Thorndike, Skinner developed the concept of "reinforcement," which is anything that occurs after a response that increases the likelihood that the response will be repeated. For example, if you want a worker to work harder and you know that he or she would like to earn extra money, then you might be able to get him or her to work harder if you give him or her a bonus for increased productivity. That means that the worker will be more likely to work harder in the future. This is called "positive reinforcement," which is about the same thing as a reward; behavior followed by a reward is more likely to be repeated. This new type of learning is called "operant (or Skinnerian) conditioning."

You can also increase the probability of a given response by removing an aversive stimulus, and this is called negative reinforcement. For example, if I teach a rat to press a handle and it gets a food pellet, it will continue to press the handle to get the reward (positive reinforcement).

However, if I give a different rat a small shock and it can turn the shock off by pushing the handle, it will learn very quickly to press the handle; this is negative reinforcement. Skinner also points out that punishment seems like the opposite of reinforcement because you are trying to decrease a response and you can do this by adding something negative or removing something positive. Skinner, however, points out that punishment is not exactly the opposite of reinforcement because it does not always work, it may create negative reactions, and the effects are unstable. Therefore, he felt that if you wanted to remove a response, you should simply find out what is reinforcing the response and eliminate the stimulus that is the reinforcer and that when the reinforcement stops, so will the behavior—this is called "extinction."

There is a type of program in Industrial/Organizational Psychology (the area that primarily deals with work behavior) called organizational behavior modification (OB Mod), and this is primarily an application of operant conditioning to the workplace. It is a way of systematically using reinforcement and extinction to foster more positive and productive work behavior and eliminate unwanted or dysfunctional work behaviors. There have been some very impressive examples of the application of OB Mod in the development of training programs and reward programs that allow employees to obtain higher levels of reward in response to changes in their behavior. Even if there is not a specific program in place, whenever we try to improve worker performance by systematically reinforcing specific types of behavior, we are using operant conditioning. Too often, managers and supervisors think that rewards simply mean more money, but research has demonstrated that although people want and expect to be paid fairly, the rewards that mean a lot to them are things like recognition, new opportunities, getting helpful and encouraging feedback, and many other things that do not cost any money but are very helpful and desirable anyway.

Albert Bandura

It was clear that classical conditioning did not explain all human learning, and when Skinner developed operant conditioning, this added new dimensions to learning and could explain even more about how people learned new behaviors. However, it was obvious that even with the new model of conditioning, there was still a significant amount of learning that was not explained by either classical or operant conditioning. A behavioral psychologist from Stanford University, Albert Bandura, started examining how complex behaviors were learned, and he could see that some learning occurred cognitively (through perception and thinking) and that people could learn some behaviors without ever having had to do them. He developed an alternative to the older models of learning, and although he did not disagree with either of them, he felt that by adding what he called Social Learning Theory, much more of human learning could be explained. For example, learning language is clearly more complex than simply looking at the stimulus-response relationships or what the reinforcers are. There appear to be aspects of our brains that equip us for learning language more easily, and it is obvious that much of language learning occurs by observation (or modeling). Bandura found that many complex human behaviors like altruism, courtesy, manners, and so forth were largely acquired by observational learning, but he also found that even negative things like aggression, smoking, using drugs and alcohol, and others were also frequently learned, at least in part, by observation.

It is easy to see how Social Learning Theory applies to the workplace, and this is one of the reasons why consultants and researchers point out to managers and supervisors that if they want employees to work hard and be ethical, then they need to be the role models who provide the examples of the kinds of behavior that is expected of workers.

Summary of Behavioral Theories

The behavioral approach has provided many techniques that have been helpful in training and managing employees, and when applied consistently and ethically, these types of techniques can be very helpful. One of the most important elements of the behavioral theories is that they have been grounded in research and experimentation that has made it easier to find what kinds of things work and what do not. These approaches have not been based on speculation and logic but on rigorous scientific research.

HUMANISTIC AND EXISTENTIAL THEORIES

This type of theory is somewhat like the psychodynamic approaches because they focus on things that go on inside the person's mind. However, unlike most of the psychodynamic theories, both the humanistic and the existential theories do not look at behavior as being primarily determined by unconscious forces or external stimuli, but rather they attribute human thoughts, feelings, and actions to more conscious processes and look at factors like free will and freedom of choice as basic characteristics of the human condition.

Humanism is a philosophical approach that believes that human nature and humanity are fundamentally good and worthwhile. These theorists also suggest that humanism is a progressive approach to life that confirms our ability and responsibility to lead ethical and meaningful lives and that all people can and should make positive contributions to society and culture. This approach to psychology is very positive and optimistic, considers human beings to be healthy and good, and when people do unhealthy, unethical, or evil things, it is because the environment and society have corrupted their human nature.

Existentialism is another philosophical approach to understanding people and how they function. In many ways, this is similar to humanism, and they are frequently grouped together as similar approaches. Some would say that existentialism is a philosophy that is concerned with a person finding his or her true self and the meaning of his or her life through the exercise of free will, choice, and personal responsibility. This perspective is not interested in the "causes" of behavior but rather on the choices that a person makes to try to become the individual that he or she would hope to be; the emphasis is on choice and responsibility. There are a number of psychologists and psychiatrists who have had a significant impact on personality theories, and although most of these are more historically relevant than mainstream today, their contributions and ideas about things like work are worth exploring.

Erich Fromm

Erich Fromm received a PhD in sociology and then went on to be trained in classical psychoanalysis in Berlin. He was from Germany but later came to the United States for further study and training and eventually had a private practice in New York. He was married to noted psychoanalyst Frieda Fromm-Reichmann, and when she died, he married Karen Horney, and they later separated. He moved to Mexico where he taught, trained others, and conducted therapy and had a major influence on Mexican psychology. He then moved to Switzerland where he spent the last few years of his life.

Fromm was considered to be a "Neo-Freudian" as were others who broke away from the traditional Freudian approaches and theory, and he is considered to be one of the early "bridges" between psychoanalysis and Humanistic Psychology. Certainly, because of his background in sociology, and also because of the influence of his two wives (particularly Karen Horney), his theory and approach to therapy were much more socially oriented than traditional psychoanalysis. He also was considered to be a social philosopher and was very aware of the political and social implications of his theory and ideas.

One of the fundamental elements of his theory is that people feel lonely and isolated because we have become separated from nature and from other human beings. Although he would see work as a traditional human activity, he also would think of work as a way that people could fulfill their needs and aspirations that would enable them to live a fuller and more rewarding life but would also unify them with other workers who were seeking to fulfill their needs while benefiting the rest of society. Thus, he was very interested in people's relations to one another, and also how they related to society and became productive members of their relevant social reference groups, and contributed to the benefit of society as a whole.

Abraham Maslow

Maslow was a very popular psychologist in the 1950s–1970s and was primarily known for his theory of motivation. Of course, he did talk about many other elements of human psychology besides motivation, but that was the basis of his whole approach. Maslow had significant differences with many of the theorists of his era for many reasons. First, he felt that strictly deterministic theories like psychoanalysis and behaviorism were too narrow in their conception of human psychology. Although he did agree that some behavior was determined by knowable causes, he also believed that people have free will and can make choices that will alter or change their outcomes and future. He believed that any theory that did not allow for free will and choice was missing one of the fundamental bases of what it meant to be human. He also argued that most theories of personality, like Freudian psychoanalysis for example, were developed by studying "abnormal" cases—that is, people seeking treatment for psychological conditions. Maslow thought that personality should be explored from the standpoint of studying the positive and best aspects of being human. His popular and somewhat "counterculture" approach was so popular among students, mental health professionals, and other psychologists that he was even elected as president of the American Psychological Association.

According to Maslow, all people have a "pyramid" of needs that are common to all people and are arranged in an order that is universal for all people. At the bottom of the pyramid are the physiological needs like food, water, warmth, and rest, and these must be met, at least minimally, before the next level of needs becomes relevant. The second level includes the safety and security needs, and after the physiological needs are met, the safety and security needs become the most important. When these needs are met, our social needs like belongingness and love become most important, and we are primarily motivated to meet these types of needs. The next level includes the esteem needs, and this means that we have basic need to feel good about ourselves and to have others feel good about us as well. Finally, at the top of the pyramid are the self-actualization needs, and this, according to Maslow, means that each of us has inside of us the drive to become the very best "us" of which we are capable. Where we get into trouble psychologically is when we are trying to satisfy others instead of paying attention to our own needs and trying to be conscientious about fulfilling them responsibly and as completely as possible.

Maslow's theory has been applied to the work setting many times and has been used to study work motivation for decades. There are certainly more recent theories that are much more supported by the research literature, but Maslow's theory is easy to understand and apply, and thus, it remains popular in the organizational setting. It is interesting to note that most union contracts apply primarily to the two bottom levels of the pyramid—that is, the most basic needs. However, considerable research has demonstrated that many workers are most often motivated by the higher-level needs, but this also assumes that the lower-level needs are at least reasonably met. This is a problem in many organizations today when salaries may be low and workers cannot support their families without a second income, and if they do not have adequate benefits like health insurance, this means that they cannot be motivated by the higher-level needs because the most basic ones are not being met. Similarly, if workers do not feel that they have reasonable job security and that they could be laid off or their job sent overseas, then they are not likely to be motivated by the higher-level needs. If the highest need is self-actualization and many (perhaps most) workers are not even getting their basic needs met, it is very unlikely that most workers will have the opportunity to self-actualize, at least in their profession. Further, with the tendency in many organizations to force people into early retirement or lay them off when they get older, that means that at the age when workers used to look forward to being respected and valued for their skills and contributions (which would help fulfill esteem and self-actualization needs), they are being shuffled aside and replaced by younger, cheaper, and less experienced workers.

Clearly, Maslow's theory does have some implications for the psychology of work, and this is one of the reasons why this theory is still around. It is interesting that Maslow's ideas seem to make sense in trying to understand some of the motivational bases of why people work, but most organizations do not appear to pay much attention to these ideas.

Carl Rogers

One of Maslow's contemporaries was Carl Rogers who was committed to applying more humanistic ideas to the field of psychology, and he, too, was very popular and was also elected president of the American Psychological Association. Many of his ideas were like Maslow's, and they two of them were thought of as being very similar. For example, Rogers, too, was interested in how people can self-actualize and fulfill their needs and desires in positive and constructive ways. Although Maslow focused on human motivation, Rogers was more interested in the "self," which he considered to be the core of a person's personality. For a person to be fulfilled and happy, it is important that his or her experiences are consistent with his or her self. It is when a person's experiences and life are "out of sync" with their self that they begin to have psychological difficulties.

Since he felt that all people have an inner sense of what is right for them (he calls this the innate valuing tendency), they should consistently pursue activities and experiences that are consistent with what their "inner self" feels is right for them. The problem emerges when we also try to satisfy another need—the need for positive regard. This means that we need to feel good about ourselves and we also need others to feel good about us. However, if others expect things of us that are not in our best interest, then we start developing "conditions of worth," which means we feel that if others are to value us, then we need to do what they want and ignore what we think is best for us. For example, a person might want to be an artist but everyone in his or her family thinks he or she should be an engineer; if we continually disregard our inner needs and desires, ultimately this will create difficulties for us psychologically.

Rogers's ideas about people and work are very like Maslow's, but the basic thing that is probably most important is that he would encourage people to pursue work that is meaningful and rewarding for them if they truly want to self-actualize. He would also encourage businesses and organizations to make sure that workers can accomplish their job effectively, in ways that allow them to pursue their own goals and aspirations as well. As mentioned with Maslow, as good as this sounds, it is not particularly compatible with the workplace today—at least in most organizations. More frequently in many organizations, individual employees are looked at as interchangeable pieces in a big machine, and thus, the idea of individual expression and goals is not as frequently considered as it might be.

Rollo May

Originally trained in divinity, May spent a couple of years as a pastor and then went back to school and became a clinical psychologist. His main contribution to his new field was to integrate classical existentialism (a branch of philosophy) into mainstream psychology. Many of his concerns about American psychology were very like the humanistic psychologists, and he felt that we needed to introduce more of the essential features of being an independent and active human being into psychology, which he and others felt was becoming too reductionistic and tied to very narrow conceptions of what it means to be a person. He emphasized the vital importance of making choices (using free will) and assuming responsibility for ourselves. If people understand themselves, their history, their circumstances, and their needs and goals and have the courage to make decisions with these things in mind, then they have a chance to experience freedom and become a self-fulfilled and "whole" person. Freedom involves risk and may produce uncertainty and even anxiety, but exercising our freedom and accepting the consequences of our choices and actions is what May felt were essential for all of us to grow into the people we can become.

The basic contribution of May with respect to the world of work is very like the humanists and involves people making choices about their lives, accepting the consequences, moving forward, and growing into a more complete and mature person. These ideas probably make the most sense at the phase of one's career when they are deciding what they want to do and what type of career path they want to pursue. However, we are all faced with choices and opportunities throughout our lives, and to approach them with the goal of becoming a more complete and better person is something that all of us can do throughout our lives.

THE COGNITIVE APPROACH

Many of the newer approaches to psychology focused on consciousness, thinking, perception, and reasoning. However, traditional behaviorism still focused primarily on studying overt (observable) behavior. As popular and influential as the behavioral approach has been, the work by Bandura opened the door to considering more cognitive types of models to help more fully understand human behavior. There have been cognitive types of theories throughout the history of psychology, but they have become more accepted and influential in the past few decades. These theories look at human personality and behavior from the standpoint of cognitive (mental) processes like perception, thinking, learning, reasoning, creativity, morality, and so forth. Like the other types of theories, we will examine just a few that represent some of the more pivotal and important contributions.

George Kelly

Many feel that Kelly is the "father" of cognitive psychotherapy and developed one of the more complete cognitive theories of personality. Of course, philosophers and others have considered cognitive elements as part of understanding people, but few of these earlier ideas would be considered complete theories. Kelly focused on the ways that people anticipate events and how they construe them when they happen. Perception and thinking were two of the most basic processes according to Kelly, and these determine not only how people process information but also how they act on information and how they feel about things that they experience.

From the standpoint of the psychology of work, cognitive elements are very important. We can certainly see how perception can influence people's attitudes about their work, the organization, and their colleagues and supervisors as well. It is also true that much of the training and work that people do depends on how they think and learn, and therefore, the cognitive anticipation, processing, and evaluation of information have much to do with cognitive factors, and Kelly was one of the first theorists to demonstrate how vitally important cognitive processes are in understanding how people function—including work.

Julian Rotter

Rotter's work has been enormously influential, and he was particularly important in bridging the gap between traditional behavioral learning theory, Social Learning Theory, and cognitive theory. Like Bandura, his approach is basically a Social Learning Theory, but because he dealt with such important cognitive elements, we will put him in this category. One of his primary ideas was the notion of behavior potential—that is, the likelihood of engaging in a behavior in each situation. From Rotter's perspective, you cannot understand a behavior without also considering the situation in which it occurs. Similarly, one cannot look at behavior as an automatic response to a specific stimulus—each person is different, and it is the interaction between the person and the situation that will result in a specific behavior.

Rotter also talked about the importance of expectancy—that is, the subjective probability that a behavior will result in a specific outcome. This adds a cognitive element to traditional operant conditioning and the notion of reinforcement, because it is not just the addition of a reinforcer that will determine behavior but that the behavior will occur because the person in question *expects* that the behavior will result in a reinforcer. Further, the subjective value of the reinforcer is also important because how important a given reinforcer is for the person will determine both his or her expectancy and the likelihood that he or she will engage in the specific behavior.

One of the most important of Rotter's contributions was the idea of "locus of control" of reinforcement. This variable has been widely used in research and is one of the more commonly used factors in research done in the workplace. Locus of control refers to a person's perception of the cause of behavior—theirs or other people's. Internal locus of control means that the person feels that behavior is largely due to the person himself or herself, whereas external locus of control means that it is perceived that a person's behavior is primarily due to external factors. If a student does well on an exam and explains his or her performance by saying that he or she is a good student and that he or she studied very hard, then he or she is demonstrating internal locus of control. However, if the same student does poorly on an exam and explains his or her performance by saying that the exam was unfair and that the professor has it in for him or her, then he or she is demonstrating external locus of control. Note that the idea of locus of control does not deal with what the actual reality is, but rather what is the person's perception of the cause of behavior.

There are hundreds of studies that look at locus of control in work settings and how this affects the behavior of workers and supervisors. For example, people with high internal locus of control are more likely to benefit from training, to take on responsibility, and to respond more favorable to feedback. This sounds like organizations should only hire people with high internal locus of control, but this is not true because it neglects one of Rotter's fundamental ideas—the importance of the interaction of the person with the situation. Thus, if you want workers to act more like people with internal locus of control, then they should be given opportunities to take control of various elements in their job, they should be given meaningful feedback, and good performance should be recognized and rewarded. Another way to look at this is that if you want people to act as if they can control their own behavior, they must have the opportunity to exert this kind of control.

Rotter's work has been widely used in Industrial/Organizational Psychology and has had a significant impact on the work environment. His blend of behavioral and cognitive psychology, his emphasis on the importance of research, and his focus on cognitive factors like expectancy and locus of control has been enormously important.

Walter Mischel

Mischel has had a very important impact on modern psychology. In the face of evidence purporting to demonstrate the importance of traits and other types of individual differences as ways of understanding and predicting behavior, Mischel took the controversial position of insisting the behavior is better explained and predicted by looking at the situation in which the behavior occurs instead of looking at the traits and personality of the individual. As clearly and convincingly as Mischel's case was, it was also clear that no two people will react *exactly* the same in the similar situation, although it is also true that the situation is still a better predictor of behavior than the personality of the individual. Clearly, it is accepted by most psychologists that you cannot understand or predict behavior without considering the context of that behavior, and yet we still must account for individual differences in the situations as well; therefore, neither factor is sufficient on its own, but both are necessary to truly understand behavior. This interactionist position describes what most psychologists believe today, and Mischel was a big part of bringing that perspective into the mainstream of psychology today. We classify Mischel as a cognitive type of theorist because he emphasizes the importance of how a person processes and interprets situational cues as providing some ideas about why someone will act in certain ways in each situation; however, his interactionist position is his major contribution.

From a work perspective, Mischel's position has some very interesting implications. If managers and supervisors want to better control and predict worker behavior, the best way is to take advantage of the things that they have most control over. For example, being a good role model, recognizing and rewarding good work behavior, providing adequate training and support, giving consistent and helpful feedback, having a safe and supportive work environment, and offering appropriate wages and benefits are examples of things that managers and supervisors can control in the situation. However, they can also have impact of the worker directly by making sure that they are hiring the best workers that they can get for the job in question. By doing these types of things, the organization can be sure that they are doing the most that they can to be productive and efficient.

SUMMARY AND CONCLUSION

There are many ways to think about the psychological role of work in people's lives, and in this chapter, we examine some of them. Of course, there are hundreds, even thousands, of psychologists who have written about and done research about work. I have tried to provide a broad view of a variety of different perspectives and given examples of some of the notable psychologists who have provided some insight into the psychological importance of work. As mentioned earlier, rather than trying to decide which of these theories is "right," it will be more productive for you to find bits and pieces of each theory that you find helpful and putting together your own "theory" about the psychology of work. If this helps you understand work in general and the importance of work in your life, then this might be very helpful for you now and/or in the future.

5

When: Work throughout the Life Cycle

It seems clear that people will approach work differently at various ages and that people from different generations will look at work from somewhat distinctive perspectives. To examine the psychological world of work from a developmental perspective means that we will consider how people change over their lives and how these changes impact how, when, and why they work. We can look at younger people who work so that they can afford a car and their own apartment or perhaps to save for college or other kinds of training. This is quite different than young adults trying to establish themselves professionally and financially and/or starting and supporting a family. In their middle years, people will see work very differently than before and will also even see differences between themselves and others in their age groups; when a person reaches retirement age, work will mean something different once again.

When studying work developmentally, we will examine two different processes and comparisons. First, we may want to look at how people in different ages approach work and compare them to one another *at the same point in time* (the cross-sectional approach). The second way to explore age differences is to follow a person or group throughout their working life and see how they change over time with respect to their job (the longitudinal approach). When we examine workers from different generations, we can usually see that they feel and act differently regarding their jobs.

However, even though there may be differences between age groups as to how they deal with work, there are also considerable differences between people within any single age group. What most of the studies have tried to do is to describe a common or "average" characteristic that might describe many or most of the people within an age group, but no single characteristic besides age will describe everyone in a specific age group. Most researchers and writers today talk about four different generations that are represented in our worker population today. We will look at each of them and see how they differ and how they fit into the workplace today.

GENERATIONS IN THE WORKFORCE

Traditionalists

Those born before and during World War II make up about 5 percent of the workforce and tend to be conventional in their values and usually are more conforming and likely to follow rules and social expectations. This generation tends to think about their role in contributing to the whole of society and is dedicated and willing to sacrifice for others' benefit. They are willing to work hard and delay their rewards in exchange for security and safety. It is common for these people to be savers, be family oriented, place duty before pleasure, be loyal and dedicated, and be patriotic and trust the government.

For this generation, probably the major things that affected them were the Great Depression and the two world wars, and even if all of them did not live through these events, their parents did. However, they also dealt with the Korean conflict, the Vietnam War, and the Cold War too; this generation lived most of their lives either in a major war or fearing that one was just around the corner. They also saw the birth of the Atomic Age and massive weapons of mass destruction and witnessed the birth of the Space Age. Although for many in this generation, their early lives might have been difficult and even marked by significant hardship, they also lived to see the postwar boom in prosperity.

In terms of their personal characteristics, they work hard and are usually committed to their company and its leadership; further, they pride themselves on being competent and doing a good job. Traditionalists have a strong work ethic and tend to be task oriented. Honor is very important to this generation, and they pride themselves on being respected and trusted. They are often perceived as being good employees because they abhor waste, are conscientious and loyal, and are willing to follow the rules and to obey authority.

This generation looks at the nuclear family as the foundation of society and values the connection with their history and extended family. While they value education, they grew up with higher education being largely a dream and expected to work hard and progress through the ranks to have a job with a good organization that treats them well, pays them fairly, and one of which they can be proud. For these employees, it is expected that most of what you need to know about your job will be learned at work. Although they are adaptable and can learn to use technology, they often find that dependence on the new technology and social media is misplaced, and they find that some of the use of electronic media is intrusive and rude.

While this age group is the most likely to be loyal to their company, they have difficulty understanding why companies do not support and value older workers. They came through most of their working life in a system that valued seniority and experience, and to see how little job security there is compared to past years is very troubling to them. Having worked their whole life to support their family and provide for retirement, it is hard for them to understand how some of the younger generations are so "me-oriented" and think so little of others. This generation also frequently has difficulty adapting to retirement, and it is true that most of the full-time workers in the Traditionalist Generation were males; women may have worked, but they were not usually the primary financial support for the family, and thus, retirement is not as often as big a problem for them as it is for men.

In general, these people are very responsible and expect others to honor their commitments and to act responsibly as well. It is upsetting to them to see how values like honesty, trust, faithfulness, respect, self-control, and hard work mean so little to others they may work with. They also grew up with the idea that you would have coworkers whom you would spend most of your working life with, and these people were expected to be a primarily important social reference group in their lives. They expect to be treated fairly and truly value due process and fair play.

The work environment that the traditionalists prefer is conservative and hierarchical. They respect the chain of command and expect top-down management. For them, work is an obligation that they take seriously, and they anticipate a long-term career with an organization that they perceive as being somewhat paternalistic—one that will take care of them. Job security and stability are very important to them, and they expect that from their organization. They value history and tradition and want to be associated with a company with a good reputation for treating employees fairly and ethically. They are more comfortable with clearly defined rules and policies and take these things very seriously.

As many positive aspects this group has as workers, traditionalists have some liabilities as well. For example, they tend to have difficultly adapting to changes and do not deal well with ambiguity and uncertainty. Their approach to authority is very hierarchical and based on a military-like chain of command. They tend to avoid conflict and look at many issues as "black-white" or "right-wrong"—they do not like the "gray" parts of situations or conflicts.

Communication with traditionalists is preferred to be discrete, formal, and logical. They respond well to being treated with respect for their age and experience—for example, being addressed as Mr., Mrs., or Miss. They also appreciate good grammar and manners and do not appreciate profanity in formal conversation, nor do they like having their time wasted with casual conversation—they want to be left alone to do their job. They do like being perceived as part of the team/group and not singled out. They are usually slow to warm up and tend to be somewhat reserved in their communication and conversations. Typically, they prefer personal communications like memos and handwritten notes as well as personal interaction.

With respect to feedback and rewards, these workers are generally of the "no news is good news" generation. For them, satisfaction at work comes from doing their job well. Feedback is valued if it is personal, meaningful, and respectful. They are motivated primarily by being valued and respected as well as job security, and they look at wages and benefits as what they expect for their livelihood in recognition for doing a good job. In terms of work/family life balance, they tend to have strict boundaries— "never the twain shall meet." They like to keep the different parts of their lives separate and expect that after working for most of their lives, they should get a fair pension that will allow them to focus on the balance in the rest of their lives.

Baby Boomers

"Boomers" are those born between 1946 and 1964 and are presently the largest generation in the workplace today. This group of people grew up with the Civil Rights Movement, the Vietnam War, the Sexual Revolution, the Cold War with the Soviet Union, and the reality of space travel. They also have the highest divorce and second marriage rate in history. Interestingly, this generation of hippies and radicals in the 1960s and 1970s became the Yuppies (young, upwardly mobile professionals) of the

1980s. When they were growing up in post–World War II era, they were promised the American Dream, and they vigorously pursued it. Therefore, they are often seen and described as greedy, materialistic, and ambitious; further, they questioned everything, did not trust the older generations, and felt that they were going to make the world a better place.

Many in the baby boom generation were antiwar, antigovernment, and emphatically supportive of equal rights and equal opportunities; they believed that if you wanted something badly enough and worked for it, anything was possible. They were/are optimistic and invested in social causes and community/educational issues. They were very involved with their children's needs and did whatever they could to make sure that their children had all that they needed and all the opportunities that they could imagine.

Boomers are very oriented toward personal growth and gratification and tend to be a "spend now and worry about it later" group; they value success as the basis for their sense of personal worth. They are very concerned about aging and health issues and do everything they can to keep looking and acting younger if they can.

This is an interesting generation of contrasting attributes; they manage crises well and are ambitious, but they also tend to be antiestablishment and are not afraid to challenge authority—including their "conservative" parents. They are very educated compared to earlier generations and see education as their "birthright"; they are competent and competitive and are very consumer oriented—they want to have a lot of "stuff." They also tend to value ethics, are very idealistic, and are usually good communicators. This generation also tends to "live to work" and is very loyal to their careers and employers. The boomers somewhat "invented" multitasking and pride themselves on how many things they can get done. When they were younger, they found their worth in their work ethic, but as they are getting older, they now seek a healthier work-life balance, although they still have a strong work ethic and are willing to take on responsibility.

As workers, they are driven and pride themselves on being "workaholics" and see nothing wrong with a 60-hour workweek. They seem to feel that by working long hours, they can prove their personal worth, and they see the careers as a vitally important piece of their identity and personal fulfillment. In addition, they also value quality in their work and efforts and see that as an important thing to try to attain—they tend to be "results oriented"—get the job done and do it well. When they were younger, boomers tended to question authority and even challenge it, but as they get older, they tend to be more like traditionalists—time equals authority; that is, the older you are, the more responsibility you should have. This is one group that has not focused as much on work-life balance. They were often afraid to take time off for fear of "losing their place" in the corporate line of succession. Thus, they often sacrificed family time trying to be more successful. This generation tried to do more for their children by giving them more things and opportunities; in fact, they probably gave their children more of everything except their time.

Typically, these people do not like conformity and rules and may question authority, but they do see work as an anchor in their lives and are team- and process oriented, which means that their work colleagues are very important as social elements in their lives, and they tend to be relationship focused at work. It is their preference to have a warm and friendly work environment; they prefer democratic processes, tend to be humane, and seem to truly be committed to equal opportunities for all. Unlike the traditionalists, they favor the "flatter" organizational hierarchy rather than the militaristic, direct line of authority that is "top-down" and more autocratic. Taking risks is something they are not afraid of, and they tend to work very efficiently. They are very aware of the importance of "youthfulness," and although this is important to them, they also expect respect from younger workers.

Boomers think of their jobs as a career and even an adventure, and they expect to work hard and then retire; however, many of them find second careers or continue working past retirement. They do like to think of themselves as contributors and even "stars," and it is important to them to see their company as ethical and standing up for the "right" things. They work well in teams and appreciate accomplishments that they and others feel good about.

In terms of their work assets as employees, they want very badly to please their superiors and colleagues and will work very hard to accomplish this goal. They tend to be mission oriented and are good at seeing the big picture and breaking complex goals down into specific tasks. They want to please others, but they will challenge authority to try to improve things. However, they also do not like conflict, and they are very aware of "political correctness" and how to manage a political environment. They will work hard and "go the extra mile" to get things done right.

On the other hand, boomers also have their liabilities as workers; for example, they are often "workaholics," and they expect others to be the same way. While they may challenge the status quo, they do not like conflict or change that they have not initiated. They are often self-centered, tend to have strong feelings about things, and may be judgmental of those who disagree with them, but they are also very loyal to peers whom they feel they are close to.

With respect to communication, boomers like to deal with people directly and face-to-face, and they are diplomatic and appreciate working closely with people. They use communication well and use body language and "rich" communication media. They tend to be technically adept but prefer talking "with" people rather than texting or using social media. They like to have options and do not like to be taken for granted, ordered around, ignored, and not listened to and will get resistant when they feel that they are being manipulated. They like the "personal touch" from managers, are comfortable being on a first-name basis with superiors and subordinates, and expect to be consulted and included in consensus-type of decisions. They respond well when they understand the organizational mission and how they fit into that and can contribute. Although they do feel rewarded by financial incentives, they very much like praise, title recognition, visible awards (something to hang on the wall), and getting awards and notice from others for all their hard work.

This is not a generation with a good work-life balance, and they basically live to work, and as they get older, they are starting to look for things like flexible hours and want more balance in their lives. However, they are also not as financially conscientious as earlier generations, and they may now worry that they do not have enough money for a comfortable retirement and may continue working to keep their standard of living intact.

Generation X

This generation of Americans was born between 1965 and 1979 and has been called Gen X, Xers, postboomers, and the 13th Generation. They grew up with Watergate, the energy crisis, dual income families, single parents, and blended families and were the first generation of latchkey kids and the first to frequently be in day care and preschool. They also lived through the Y2K, corporate downsizing, the end of the Cold War, most moms working, and an increase in the divorce rate. Their perceptions have been shaped by being on their own and taking care of and entertaining themselves, and seeing computers and cell phones become part of the American scene. They also watched continuing examples of politicians lying, parents getting laid off, and corporations being flagrantly unethical and sometimes unlawful. This generation was the first to see America starting to lose status as the most powerful and prosperous nation in the world, and although they may not realize it, this is the first generation in modern American history that will probably not do as well financially as their parents.

Their values are quite different from their parents, who had been very different than their parents as well. Xers want balance and diversity in their lives and are more focused on having fun than working all the time. They tend to be entrepreneurial and willing to try new things, and they are well educated and have very high job expectations. This generation frequently feels that they should not have to start at the bottom and work their way up, but that they should be able to start their adult lives at very much the same level as their parents are now. They tend to be very informal and somewhat pragmatic if also a little unrealistic in their goals and aspirations. As a group, they are more focused on themselves and have little in the way or organizational loyalty and dedication. Self-reliance is a trait that many of them have, but they frequently suffer from a sense of entitlement that may be unwarranted, which leads them to be skeptical and cynical about others; they tend to not trust or believe in the values of their boomer parents. They are also much more likely to be technically savvy and to think globally.

In terms of their personal attributes, this group presents many different and sometimes conflicting values and attributes. Although they are self-reliant, independent, and adaptable, they are finding that things are not as easy for them as they expected them to be, and this leads them to have antiestablishment attitudes and be frequently angry without understanding why. They think of themselves as principled and ethical, but they are usually flexible and consider themselves to be "free agents," and although they do not trust leadership or many people in the boomer generation, they do tend to trust some people (including managers) even though they may not see themselves as loyal to their organizations. This generation has the highest percentage of divorced parents, and they were frequently pampered as children. They will take on responsibility and tend to be results-driven. Rather than being like the boomers who lived to work, Xers tend to work to live. They do tend to be better with money than their parents and are more financially conservative.

As workers, they do not like overtime, and they do not want to be like their "workaholic" boomer parents. They want balance in their lives and do not seem to mind if they lose their place on the corporate ladder because they take some time off work. They like structure and clear expectations, but they tend not to trust authority and are somewhat skeptical and will test authority repeatedly. More than their work ethic, they want to be valued for their skills, and they expect that their skill set will (and should) lead them to success. They do like a casual work environment, and they want meaningful work and the chance to be innovative. At work, they prefer diversity, technology, informality, and fun. They rely on their technological acuity and business savvy to stay marketable and do not mind changing jobs when it suits them. They may be criticized for not having an attachment or commitment to an employer, but they seem to want to move in, get the job done, and move on to the next thing.

In terms of their assets as workers, Xers adapt well to change and thrive on flexibility, are eager to learn, are very determined, and manage tasks well. Typically, they have a "consumer mentality," which can be very helpful to many jobs. They communicate directly and are clear in their communications and expectations. This generation tends to be highly educated, are multitaskers, not intimidated by authority, have good short-term problem-solving skills, and like feedback.

However, as a group, they also have their liabilities. They have a "portable" résumé and are always looking for the next, better job. It is common for them to be cynical and skeptical and to dislike and not trust authority; they will reject rules if the rules do not suit them. Although they can be good communicators, they often lack people skills and seem to feel that "manners" are silly and they should be able to do what they want to do. Although they are good at managing short-term goals, they often lack the ability or interest in developing a long-term outlook on things and want the quick payoff—they are usually impatient; they see the optimism of their parents and other generations as naïve.

Millennials

The latest generation to enter the workforce is the millennials—those born between 1980 and 1994. They are also referred to as Generation Y, Gen Y, Generation Next, echo boomers, and 24/7s. They grew up with digital media, a child-focused world, school shootings, AIDS, 9/11, and terrorist attacks. Very frequently, they are children of divorce, single parents, blended families, and two-career parents. Interestingly, they hope to be the "next great generation" and reverse all the wrong they see in the world. This generation grew up as the most sheltered of any other group as their parents tried to protect them from the evils of the world. They came of age during a period of economic expansion and have come to expect a lot from the world. As children they were kept very busy and frequently had schedules that they were expected to keep.

The values that seem most important to millennials involve achievement, confidence, and civic duty. They are very technically savvy and are avid consumers expecting that they *must* have the very latest of whatever new phone or gadget is available, and they feel that this is an essential right that they have regardless of the socioeconomic background of their family. Diversity is a given for many or most of this generation, and they frequently consider themselves to be members of a global community.

In fact, it is common for this group to count as close friends people in other countries whom they have never met except through social media. Although they are very sociable, they do rely heavily on social media and electronic communication. As a group, they tend to have high moral values and are more spiritual than other generations. However, that does not mean that they are likely to actively involve with formal religious groups; they seem more "street smart" than other groups, and although optimistic, they also tend to be realistic. They are the most educated generation, but they also like and expect lots of fun, including extreme fun, and are willing to take risks just to have some fun and expect that they deserve to have their enjoyment NOW!

As a group, millennials are ambitious but not always focused, and although fiercely independent, they often look to the workplace to help them find direction and pursue their goals. They are loyal to their families, but not so much to their organizations, and they are very attached to their gadgets and social media. Having been doted on for most of their lives, they have very high expectations for themselves and particularly since they are the best educated generation and are very confident; interestingly, the older generations tend to look at the quality of the education of millennials as inferior to that of earlier groups.

Millennials typically have a "me first" attitude at work, although they are very sociable, work well in teams, and are loyal to their peers. They see their parents as "heroes" unlike the Xers or boomers, and they will often see the older generations as "cool." However, they are also the most "doted upon" group when they were children, and they have a very strong sense of entitlement. Impressive titles do not impress them, but superior skills do. Often the skills they most value are technically based or involve significant risk. Thus, rather than taking guitar lessons to learn to play the guitar, they might spend many hours learning to play "Guitar Hero." They might be an expert in video games that involve real sports like baseball, football, basketball, soccer, and the like and seem to think that this is like having skills in the sport itself. Finally, this group more than any of the previous three are more patriotic (at least after 9/11), and they hope to make contributions to the world and make it a better place.

In terms of work assets, they have a consumer mentality, they are highly educated, and they are usually very goal oriented and tenacious. They multitask quickly and seem to act as if they can text a friend, be listening to a TV show, and be having a discussion with a parent at the same time and see nothing wrong with that at all; in fact, they seem not to believe that these situations really mean that they are either not doing things as well as they need to or that they are being rude. They are certainly the generation with the most technical knowledge and experience. Millennials are often optimistic with a very positive attitude and are usually easy to get along with.

This generation is not without its work liabilities either, and those tend to be obvious when someone is working with them. They dislike menial work, think it is below them, and although they are "brain smart," they lack experience and often need structure and a lot of supervision at work. Further, they tend to lack discipline and are often impatient. Training is often something they will find boring or unnecessary, and they would rather just be told what to do and then figure it out on their own. By using video games and other online or electronic media, they have learned that they do not need instruction manuals but just need to have some time to learn what they need to know in their own way and in their own time. Although they deal well with "machines" and they are sociable, they may often lack some of the social sensitivity to deal well with people face-to-face and feel that their social media is their preferred way to spending time with their friends. Consequently, they may not be able to deal very well with complex social situations or people who are difficult. As mentioned earlier, they respect skills that people may have, but they do not necessarily respect authority or people in positions above them— if they do not respect the person's skills, then they do not respect the person.

APPROACHING WORK THROUGHOUT ONE'S LIFETIME

One would expect that a worker in his or her teens would approach and feel differently about his or her job than a person in his or her 70s. When one begins his or her working life, he or she usually has specific reasons why he or she wants to work. The person may be helping to support his or her family, trying to save money for college or training school, saving for a new car, hoping to be able to move out on his or her own, and to be more independent. In the early phases of working life, people are usually trying to gain some financial "traction" to get their lives started and to become independent and self-sufficient. Even though this might be common for people early in their careers, we would probably find the reasons to be different for early career people in the different generations. For example, when traditionalists started working, it would have been common that they would have been helping to support their families, whereas in later generations, this would have been less common. Similarly, the millennials might be working so that they can afford a new phone or computer, and this would not have been common or even possible in earlier generations. However, it is probably true that in all generations, when people started their working lives, it was very likely due to factors other than fulfilling their dreams for their future of work—they usually start working for specific reasons other than self-actualization; the first job is usually more about the paycheck than a career.

After workers get past their "first job" stage of work, the reasons why they work are usually a little different. At this point, their life responsibilities are more significant and may involve getting married, supporting a family, trying to get into a more secure career position, owning a home, and so forth. Thus, things like job security, financial stability, and benefits like health insurance become more important. One thing is very clear in looking at the different generations in the workplace today is that each of them seems to approach this stage of work life a little differently; however, there is no doubt that issues of career stability, financial security, and job benefits are important for most people in this part of their working life.

For those workers in the "middle-age" part of their careers, issues of stability are even more important. Now they are in positions where they are expecting and expected to be achieving more from their jobs and careers; they are more likely to be in positions of influence and authority and are probably earning significantly more than they were in the previous stages of their life. Job security is terribly important, but this is also a time in one's working life where they may begin to question earlier decisions and may feel that they are on the wrong track and need to consider their alternatives. Frequently, looking at new career paths usually means starting at a lower level in the new path, and this may result in a decrease in salary and benefits. For many in this stage of life, it is difficult to make a change like this because of family or other responsibilities, and some may then feel like they are on a "dead-end" track from which they will never escape. Another difficult possibility in this phase of work life is that people might be laid off or forced into early retirement, and this might mean an involuntary change that would result in decreased financial and job security. In fact, this is becoming a bigger problem for many workers today—at least in the United States.

When workers enter the "autumn" of their work life and start to think about retirement and financial security, work and job issues are very different. These people are past the point in their careers where they are thinking about achievement, promotion, and raises; now they are looking at the end of their career and supporting themselves for the future. This is also a time when many of them will be facing new medical issues, and this is a worry that they will also need to address. For those who have not adequately prepared themselves for retirement, this phase of work life may also mean finding another job that will supplement whatever they have for retirement (e.g., pension, investments, and Social Security). Almost always, jobs that people take at this stage of life mean a much lower-level job with significantly less income and usually minimal or no benefits. Since many people in this group will be eligible for Medicare and Medicaid, they may not have the same need for health insurance as when they were younger, and this is often very attractive to potential employers. Further, people in this part of life are usually more responsible about things like attendance and punctuality than many younger workers, and this too makes them appealing as workers. Of course, it is also true that many in this stage of work life will continue to work because they get bored with retirement and want to do something else that is interesting, gets them around other people, and puts some money in their pockets. This is particularly true of those in the traditionalist and baby boomer generations. Although it is easy to see how people's approach to work will differ as they enter new stages of their working lives, there are many issues that will also affect individual age groups differently as well.

SOME OF THE ISSUES IN DEALING WITH A GENERATIONALLY DIVERSE WORKFORCE

Discrimination

Although many think that discrimination is not as big an issue in the United States as it used to be, it is still with us. In fact, as the workforce becomes more diverse, there are more opportunities and more evidence of discrimination, and that goes for age discrimination as well. Most of the age-related discrimination and prejudice are related to the older workers, but the youngest workers are often victimized by discrimination as well. To clarify the differences, prejudice is an attitude—that is, how we think and feel about another person or group; discrimination is an action—how we treat or behave toward another person or group. If a person is not hired because the employer thinks that he or she is too young to do the job well, this might be evidence of prejudice and discrimination; however, if in fact the person's age is young enough that he or she legitimately could not do the job well, then this is not discrimination. It is only discrimination if the person could do the job well but he or she is not hired *only* because of his or her age. Younger workers may be discriminated against in other ways, too. For example, being unfairly underpaid because the employer thinks that he or she can get away with paying a lower salary to a younger worker who may not expect more; or, the younger worker is not paid benefits like health insurance or retirement options because the employer thinks that the younger person will not care as much about benefits, which may even be true, but it is still discrimination.

Any time that a worker is treated differently and unfairly because of his or her age, this is discrimination and it is unethical, bad management, and probably illegal. There are many companies that have been legally penalized for age discrimination and have often cost these companies millions of dollars. Even middle-aged workers can be discriminated against; for example, suppose a 40-year-old employee is not offered a training opportunity because management thinks that "middle-aged" people cannot learn this new "high-tech" stuff as well as younger employees, so why waste the money!

Of course, most age discrimination targets older workers, and this is a particularly problematic area for many reasons. In today's work environment in the United States, many companies try to keep their salary costs down by forced early retirement or layoffs of older workers to save money. If it is truly age discrimination and it can be proven, then this is illegal, and the company can (and should) be sued, which may cost much more than the salary dollars that they think they are saving. Further, as discussed earlier, the research evidence is very clear—older workers in general are more efficient and more productive than younger workers, they have more knowledge, and they are usually more loyal and committed to their companies than younger workers. However, even with all of the evidence favoring older workers, companies still seem to like the short-term benefit of saving some salary costs immediately rather than looking at the longer-term savings that lower age-related turnover will provide.

Another problem with discriminating against older workers is that every year the percentage of older people in the workforce increases, and that trend will continue for many years. Thus, with an increasingly aging workforce, there will very likely be more discrimination, more people being treated unfairly, more costly lawsuits, unnecessarily expensive turnover, more loss of skilled and loyal employees, and decreased organizational performance and profit. People today are living longer, staying healthy longer, and the "workaholic baby boomer generation" is very likely to want to continue working past retirement, thus taking jobs away from younger employees who want to find a new or better job. Age discrimination is expensive, unethical, probably illegal in most instances, and basically it is just wrong.

There is substantial evidence that there are many ways that older workers are discriminated against in all parts of the world. For example, older workers may be harassed by others because of their age or physical condition, and this may not be related to their ability to do their jobs but simply because of their age. Further, there are many examples around the world where older workers are discriminated against in the areas of education and training. For example, there are very few opportunities for older people to get further education and training unless they qualify and can use the opportunities provided for younger people. There is not much in the education/training area that targets older workers specifically. Also, many countries discriminate against older workers by not providing funding for education and training that is available to younger workers.

In the area of health care, there are numerous examples of discrimination against older people in terms of access to appropriate and timely health care. For example, in one company, two employees with the exactly same health insurance may not be able to use the same services because some may not be available to people above a certain age, and this may not have anything to do with the actual medical reasons for having a particular test, procedure, appliance, medication, or surgery; they are not permitted to have the medical care they need only because of their age. There are certainly examples of companies laying older workers off or retiring them early because their medical needs might end up costing the company more in higher health insurance costs. Both in terms of medical services and research, the funding for these activities tends to favor the younger ages. Even medical education does not focus as much on older people. In the United States, more attention is given to the diagnosis and treatment of older adults than in the past, but in many developing countries, there is very little medical education in gerontology (the study and treatment of older people). Being able to get medical insurance can also be an area that affects older people and older workers specifically. Although many older and retired people are eligible for Medicare (government health insurance for older people), there are still some who are not. Further, since Medicare does not cover all health costs, many older people cannot afford to buy "Medicare gap insurance" that helps pay for the health expenses not covered by Medicare. It is not uncommon for older people to have to make the decision to either buy food or medicine, but they cannot afford both.

Managing across Generations

Depending on the company, there may be employees from three or sometimes even four generations. Obviously, workers in different age groups do not have the same needs, abilities, motivations, interests, assets, and liabilities. Therefore, a manager cannot expect to manage each of these workers the same way. Some managers pride themselves on being fair and treating everyone the same, and although this is generally a good thing, good management also means that one recognizes, respects, and manages diversity. This is not always easy, and the more diverse the workforce (including age diversity), the more opportunities there are for misunderstandings, conflict, and differing opinions and perceptions.

One interesting trend that is becoming more common in some companies is that, particularly if there is a bargaining unit like a labor union, when layoffs occur, they will usually give preference to workers based on seniority. Thus, "last in, first out," and that as layoffs continue, the employees who are left tend to be the older ones, and if they are protected by a union contract, they cannot be laid off unfairly just because of their age. The same pattern is not, however, found in managers. In fact, many companies will put younger management trainees in entry-level management positions to give them experience. This may result in an interesting situation where the managers may largely be younger people in their 30s, and they may be managing workers whose average age is in the 40s or 50s. Another thing that makes this a potentially difficult situation is that the older workers probably know more about the job and the work group than the managers do, and yet the managers are the ones who are supposed to direct the activities of the others.

There may be a different situation in other organizations where the managers may be older and the employees may be one or two generations younger. Once again, the difficulties arise because the managers and the employees may have different goals, needs, motives, and commitment to the job and the organization. Managers often have difficulty understanding why their employees do not seem to feel that what the manager wants them to do is important, and this often leads to misunderstandings and conflict.

The main thing that needs to be done to improve the quality of management in a diverse workforce is to hire managers who have appropriate education and training to manage the workforce they will need to deal with. Managers must be technically competent in the field they are working in, or the employees will not respect them or may not even listen to them unless they must. In addition, managers must have good people skills and work effectively with individuals and groups. Beyond hiring managers who have the right kinds of education and experience, companies also need to commit themselves to training managers to deal with the kinds of situations and people they will be working with. Most companies do not take managerial training very seriously and seem to think that managers can pick up the skills for this very complex and challenging job by just jumping in and doing it. Experience and research have demonstrated that when companies invest time and money training managers, it ends up saving them considerable money because the managers are more effective, get more done, and more than make up for the time and money spent on additional training.

Another tip on how to manage effectively in an age-diverse workforce is for managers to listen to employees. Most managers spend too much time talking and not nearly enough time listening. If you want to know how to motivate an employee, just listen to him or her—the employee will tell you what is important to him or her and thus what is motivating for him or her. A good manager is like a good coach—he or she knows how to get the most out of each employee or athlete, and by doing this, the manager is also helping the employee or athlete achieve his or her own goals and be successful. My definition of management is, "Accomplishing the goals of the organization through the efforts of other people." Obviously, there is more to management than this, but ultimately, this is what management is about, and managing across age groups makes this more difficult. However, the best managers find ways to do this effectively and in the best interest of the organization and each individual employee as well.

Recruiting

Recruiting is an area where age discrimination is a real problem for many people. This usually negatively impacts older workers more than younger ones, but this is not always the case. For example, young workers may run into the problem that they are not hired for a job because they do not have experience; however, how do you get experience if no one will hire you? With older workers, the discrimination is usually about things like salary; older workers may have higher needs for salary because of prior jobs where they were well paid, and they will also have a greater need for benefits like retirement and health insurance. Younger workers will often take a lower salary just to get the job, and they may not need (or think they need) benefits to the same extent as older workers. One interesting type of discrimination against older workers is the perception that they may not be around as long because of retirement or health. However, if you have two potential employees, both of whom are qualified for a specific job and one is 25 years old and the other is 55 years old, statistically, which of them is most likely to stay in this same job for at least five years? The 55-year-old is much more likely to be a loyal employee and stay in the job longer than the younger employee.

Sometimes companies do not want to hire older workers because they may have more health problems, miss work for health reasons, and cost more money on their health insurance. As long as the potential employee is physically able to do a job, he or she cannot be denied a job because he or she *might* have more health problems in the future—this is age discrimination and it is illegal. Unfortunately, the fact that this is illegal does not stop unethical companies from finding other "reasons" for deciding not to hire an older potential employee.

It is very easy for companies to avoid age discrimination at the hiring phase of attracting new employees; you simply treat all applicants the same regardless of their age, gender, race, or any other factors unrelated to their ability to do the job. As easy as this sounds, there are still many organizations that simply do not comply with this standard.

Job Security

When we were discussing some of the characteristics of the different generations of workers, it was clear that the issue of job security is very different for the various age groups. Older workers tend to be much more concerned about job security than younger employees, and this is certainly understandable. As people get older, they may have more financial responsibilities, they may have a greater need for health insurance, and as they near retirement, their future financial security becomes a much more important issue. It is also true that the older generations of workers probably have or had parents or grandparents who lived through the Great Depression (1929–World War II) and heard many stories about how awful it was to not be able to find a job and to even put food on the table.

One of the interesting issues in job security today is that many younger workers are not as loyal to their companies as older workers; they expect to move from one job to another and see job mobility as a way of improving their salary and professional position. Further, they may not be as concerned about future financial stability as older workers, so they are not concerned about retirement funds and pensions. However, today very few organizations have pension plans as generous as they used to be, and retirement accounts are generally left up to the employee to initiate and to contribute to. Although younger workers may have very high expectations about the lifestyle "they deserve," they will be far less prepared for their retirement than their boomer parents.

It is also very important for organizations to think about job security issues as well. Organizations should try to attract, recruit, hire, train, develop, and retain the very best employees they can get. Obviously, retaining the best people should be the goal of every organization, but many still try to lay people off or retire them as they get older and more expensive. Losing that kind of talent and expertise is very costly, and turnover is a major expense for organizations, so it is truly to the advantage of all organizations and employees to take job security very seriously—it is important.

Motivation and Goal Setting

All people are different, and each person has his or her own motives and goals. It is not surprising that people in different age groups may not be motivated by the same things. For example, younger workers might be more motivated by salary level and opportunities for promotion, and older workers might be more motivated by job security and benefits. However, even within age groups, there will still be many differences between people. The more diverse the work group, the more complex the issues of motivation and goal setting. Good managers will find the best way to appeal to issues that are relevant to each individual worker as well as being cognizant of the differences between age groups. Optimally, managers should try to find ways to encourage and support workers to set goals that are meaningful and attainable and also to ensure that these goals further the mission and objectives of the organization. This is clearly a complex task and one that requires managers to be bright, creative, and well trained.

Many organizations are trying to find ways to make benefit programs fit a broad range of different groups and types of employees. One of the best types of incentive programs is one that gives employees different options as to how they would like to customize their benefit package to best meet their own needs. Although this does make things more difficult for the human resources and personnel departments, it does offer the best strategy for attracting and retaining the most superior employees, and there is substantial research support for this conclusion.

Although it is certainly more complicated in many ways for managers today, we also know more, have better technology, and have better educated and well-trained employees. Finding ways to motivate and help set goals for employees is now something that we can do better than in the past, and there is no reason that we should not do this. If we want employees to work hard and do their best, we must have reasons to make them want to do this. To satisfy their own goals and motives is always a primary interest of any employee, and the manager who can help them accomplish this while also improving the organization is not just desirable, but it is necessary.

SUMMARY AND CONCLUSION

It is hardly a surprise that people in different age groups act differently and have different interests, goals, and motives; it is how organizations respond to these differences that will determine how effective, efficient, ethical, and responsible the organization is. If we look at different organizations, it is not unusual to find one that may have four generations of workers at one time. Suppose there is a worker in his or her 70s who is healthy and still wants to work, and he or she has a coworker in his or her 50s, another in his or her 30s, and one who is in his or her late teens—this kind of diversity is not rare but presents significant challenges for organizations and managers. It is not unusual that one might find this kind of diversity in minimum wage, entry-level, fast-food, and retail types of organizations, where most of the employees are part-time. Usually part-time workers will take these types of jobs for very specific reasons. The retired person who wants to make a little extra money, the parent who wants a part-time job that lets him or her work around his or her children's school schedule, the student who wants to work after school and on weekends to make extra money, or the person who wants a second job to make some extra money—with these types of different needs and motives, it is very clear as to why organizations might need and want to hire a broad diversity of employees that will meet the needs of the organization and the needs of the workers.

As we discussed earlier, for organizations to respond most positively to the increasing diversity in the workplace, and to meet the needs of different generations of workers, it is important that they pay attention to some very important factors. First, they must have and enforce very clear and reasonable policies that establish guidelines and regulations to ensure that all employees are treated legally, ethically, fairly, and without bias based on age or any other factor unrelated to job performance. Second, they need to hire and thoroughly train managers who have the education and background to be able to manage effectively in such a complex and dynamic environment. Finally, they must have policies and a reward structure (salary and benefits) that optimally meet the broad range of employee needs that the workforce presents.

As the average age of our population increases, we will continue to have a greater percentage of older people in our population each year, and this is a trend that is common in much of the world. Couple this with the fact that with improved and improving health care around the world, we will continue to have increasing issues surrounding the reality of an aging population. This will have impact on the health care system, on Medicare and

Social Security, and certainly on the workplace. As people are living longer and staying healthy into later years, many are choosing to work past retirement age because they simply want to continue working and sometimes because of financial uncertainty. This is having and will continue to have major implications for the workplace and will affect every organization and every worker in one way or another. How we address and deal with these age-related workplace issues will have much to do with how effective organizations are as they move into the future.

6

Where: Work around the World

There is very little question but that workers and managers around the world do not act the same way in their jobs, nor do they relate the same way to their organizations. Worker behavior in organizations is influenced by many factors, including the culture of the nation they are working in, the culture of the organization in which they work, the subcultures of the work groups and teams they are part of, the colleagues and friends they work and interact with, and their own personalities. Examining some of the differences in work and work behavior around the world means trying to find some of the basic differences between workers in different cultures while keeping in mind that there is always considerable variation between workers in any culture or organization, and no single set of worker characteristics will ever explain the behavior of every single worker. However, we do know that there are real and reliable differences between different countries with respect to the psychology of work, and some of these differences are very interesting.

By "culture," we are referring to "a system of shared values and beliefs held by members of a defined group that influences the thoughts, feelings, and behaviors of all of the members of a given group. This system will define the norms, actions, and attitudes that are valued by the group, what a person must do to be successful in this group, and what must be avoided if one is to elude negative sanctions or punishment for violating the norms of the group." In recent decades, organizational theorists began working with and trying to understand "organizational culture" and how this influences the behavior or workers in various organizations. Of course, when studying workers and the workplace in different parts of the world, we also must remember that national culture has a major influence on the behavior and values of workers, so when we look at some of the differences between workers in different parts of the world, we must pay attention to both national and organizational cultures.

It is difficult to pin down culture, but we have learned much from the anthropologists, who are the behavioral scientists and who have worked most with culture, and we have taken their theories and methods and applied them to organizations and other smaller groups. One way to think about organizational culture is an analogy: "Culture is to an organization as personality is to an individual." This is a very good analogy for understanding culture—it is like the personality of a given group or organization. Usually, people in the relevant group do not even think about or notice the culture because it is so pervasive and deeply ingrained that they do not even see it. One of the best descriptions of organizational culture is, "The way we do things around here." This captures the essence of culture for most groups—everyone accepts the fact that the values and norms are "just the way things are here." Of course, no two people will react to the culture in the same way, but in organizations with a "strong" culture, there is less variation in behavior because the values and norms are obvious, expected, and enforced. In weaker cultures, on the other hand, there is more variation between the behaviors of workers because the culture is not as strongly determinative of behavior. Another important point about organizational culture is that for most people, national culture is more important in determining individual behavior than organizational culture, and this points out one of the most important factors in trying to manage a diverse workforce—the more different the people in the group, the more likely they are to have values that differ from the organization, and sometimes that will create an issue. There are some theories about cultural differences between countries, and examining these theories will help us understand how cultural differences affect people and organizations.

HOFSTEDE'S CULTURAL DIMENSIONS THEORY

Geert Hofstede is a Dutch scholar who has worked for industry as well as being a researcher and professor. He has studied and written about cultural differences since the 1960s and is recognized as one of the main influences in cross-cultural psychology; he has impacted the fields of social psychology, sociology, anthropology, and management as well. Over the years, he has revised his theory to accommodate new ideas and research, and his ideas continue to generate interest and research even today. Hofstede has identified five dimensions that define national cultures, and following the work of Minkov's World Values Survey, Hofstede added a sixth dimension—indulgence versus restraint—and all of Hofstede's dimensions are conceived as a continuum that is defined by the end points of the dimensions. It is easiest to understand the dimensions by examining the end points, and while we will give examples of cultures that typify some of the more extreme positions, it is probably true that most cultures fall in the middle range of many if not most of these dimensions.

Power Distance Index

The power distance index is a dimension ranging from low to high and reflects how a specific culture conceives of and uses power. In cultures with a high power distance, there is a clear hierarchy based on apparent power, and this is clearly established and enforced without doubt or reason. In low power distance cultures, people will question authority and attempt to distribute power "fairly."

In high power distance cultures, power is not thought of as either being good or bad but is simply a "fact" of life—some people have and deserve power and some do not. Children are taught obedience, and employees are expected to follow rules and directions without question. Education is also conceived of as based on power relationships, and thus, the teachers and professors are expected to be listened to and obeyed. In this culture, older people are very much respected as well as feared. Although cultural power differences mean that there is considerable inequality in the high power distance culture, this is expected and accepted. In these types of cultures, corruption is common and scandals are usually covered up. As expected, income distribution is very uneven and favors those in power. Interestingly, the prevailing religion(s) in such a culture is also hierarchical with people in higher positions having most of the power, and frequently there is a partnership between the church and state whereby they reinforce one another's power position.

Conversely, in low power distance cultures, it is expected that the use of power should be legitimate and power is conceived of as being good (viz., legitimate) or bad (viz., illegitimate). In this type of culture, parents tend to treat children as equals, and education is very student centered. In these cultures, older people are neither respected nor feared any more than any other person, and they too are treated as equals. When hierarchies are needed in organizations or in society, this inequality is looked at as being established for convenience and efficiency, and subordinates expect to be included and considered in decisions in organizations. Although corruption will occur, it is rare and not accepted, and political corruption will usually end a career. In these cultures, there tends to be a more even distribution of income, and the differences are based on skills and/or the importance of what a person does. Even the religions in these cultures tend to stress the equality of believers, and the priests, rabbis, and ministers are not perceived as being very different from the rest of the congregation.

Individualism versus Collectivism

This index looks at the extent to which people function in groups and strongly identify with the relevant groups of which they are a part. Societies that are more individualistic have more loose ties, and people do not strongly identify with their groups other than their immediate family; they are more likely to think of "I" rather than "we." In collectivist societies, tightly integrated relationships tie extended families and others in to tightly organized groups to which people are unquestionably loyal and expect and give support to other group members.

In individualistic societies, individuals are expected to take care of themselves and their immediate family only. They are very conscious of privacy and the rights of individuals, and they feel that speaking their mind is healthy and good for society; they feel that their voice matters and they expect to be heard. If they transgress the norms of groups of which they are a part, they might feel guilty, which is a very individual emotion. In this type of society, the word "I" is used more frequently than "we," and in groups (including work), tasks are more important than relationships. Education and training are about learning how to learn and acquiring task skills that will allow them to achieve individually.

People in collectivist societies have strong ties to extended families or clans from which they expect support and protection in exchange for unquestioned loyalty. These people typically think more in "we" terms than "I" terms, and they stress the importance of belonging rather than individual identity. They do tend to think of others in terms of "in-group" or "out-group"; that is, they think of others as being a member of the group or groups the individual feels a part of, or someone from a different and possibly competitive or hostile group. Rather than feeling guilty for wrongdoing, collectivist people are more likely to feel shame, which is an emotion based upon the perceptions and feelings of others. In this type of society, education is about learning tasks that will help society, and in work groups, relationships are more important than specific tasks.

Uncertainty Avoidance

Just as some people like to take risks and others would rather avoid risk, there are cultures that tend to be like this as well. Although no one in any culture is just like someone else on any variable, in cultures that prefer to avoid uncertainty and risk it means that "on the average" most people tend to avoid uncertainty and risk; similarly, there are also some cultures (like some individuals) that do not seem to fear uncertainty and might even enjoy taking risks.

In countries where people tend not to avoid uncertainty, they seem to accept the fact that risk is part of life, and it is an aspect of every day. These individuals often seem more at ease, exhibit lower levels of stress and anxiety, and seem to have more of a sense of self-control. Research also suggests that people in low uncertainty-avoidance cultures score higher on measures of subjective health and well-being. One interesting element of these types of cultures is that they often are more tolerant of deviance and may look at differences as interesting rather than threatening. Since they are more comfortable with ambiguity, authority figures like teachers are not afraid to say "I don't know" when they do not have an answer.

One thing that might be a work issue in this type of culture is that people tend not to like to be pinned down by rules, written or unwritten, and they are also not very worried about changing jobs or companies. With respect to morality and philosophy, people in low uncertainty-avoidance cultures tend to look at things as "relativistic," which means that they will accept moral and ethical ambiguity if there are differences based on situations or complexity. When it comes to things like science, they like empirical evidence rather than faith.

For cultures and countries that are high in uncertainty-avoidance, risk and uncertainty tend to be experienced as a continuous threat that must be fought and never accepted—they want answers and certainty. However, these people do seem to reflect higher levels of stress and anxiety and score high on measures of "neuroticism." Similarly, research indicates that they also have lower scores on tests of subjective health and well-being. As a group, these people are less tolerant of deviant behavior or ideas and perceive that differences are dangerous.

To make themselves feel more in control and more comfortable, people with high uncertainty avoidance need clarity, answers, and structure; interestingly, they do not seem to need empirical evidence for their answers if these answers reduce their sense of risk and uncertainty. They expect teachers and authorities to have the answers and do not want to hear them voice uncertainty or lack answers. Workers who live in this type of culture do not leave jobs easily and may stay with a job they hate for fear that the next one will probably be even worse. They seem to need rules and guidelines, and although these make them feel more comfortable, that does not mean that they will always follow the rules. In religion, philosophy, and science, people in these cultures believe in ultimate truths and grand theories. If scientific evidence violates their beliefs, they are quick to dismiss the science as "nonsense" and that scientists do not know what they are talking about.

Masculinity versus Femininity

This scale measures the extent to which a specific culture "in general" seems to value primarily traditional and stereotypic masculine values or leans more to the values often associated with femininity. Cultures that are more feminine in their orientation feel that social role differentiation between the genders is minimal and not very important. They also usually feel that men and women should be modest and caring and value a good balance between home and family. They also usually feel sympathetic for the weak and disenfranchised in their society. There are no expectations that men and women should be different in their experience of emotions, and they believe that men and women should deal equally with facts and emotions. In terms of emotions and aggression, these people feel that boys and girls should feel that they can cry or express emotions, but that fighting and aggression are not acceptable ways to deal with conflict. In this type of society, a woman has the right to choose whether to have children, and although men should have a voice, the ultimate decision is the woman's because she is the one who is committing her body to carry and deliver the child. Women are also expected to be politically active and involved and should be able to run for and hold political office. In terms of religion, people in more feminine cultures tend to believe that spirituality should focus on other people and one's experience of life. They usually have very "matter-of-fact" attitudes about sexuality and see sex as a normal and healthy way to relate to people whom you care about.

Masculine cultures focus more on the differences between the genders and see the social and emotional roles between men and women to be very different. Men are expected to be assertive and ambitious, and although women may be permitted to have these traits, they are still perceived to be masculine traits. In terms of work-life balance, a masculine culture usually assumes and believes that work should prevail over family, and the most important thing that a father can do is to provide for his family.

They feel that weakness is a failing, and that strength is to be sought and admired. When asked, they will state that men and fathers deal with facts and women and mothers deal with feelings; these perceptions are clearly communicated to children when they are growing up. In terms of emotions and aggression, the "rules" in masculine societies are very clear: girls cry and boys do not; boys should "fight back," but girls should not fight at all.

In this type of society, the man is the "king of the castle" and is expected to make most of the important family decisions, including the decision to have children and how many to have. Women are "allowed" to participate in politics but are not expected to run for or hold political office. Religion focuses primarily on a God-figure, and relations to other people are less important; God is also usually felt to be a masculine figure. They also tend to be very moralistic about sexuality and see sex primarily of performing acts that bring pleasure and offspring. Sex is felt to be a male's prerogative, and the woman or wife should "fulfill her sexual responsibility" to her male partner or spouse. In these cultures, sexual "double standards" are assumed to be normal and expected—by the men, at least.

Short-Term versus Long-Term Orientation

Some cultures, just like some people, tend to think and plan with long-term objectives in mind, whereas others focus more on short-term objectives and goals. For cultures that are typically more short-term oriented, they usually feel that the most important events in their lives occurred in the past or are in present situations. They also focus on stability and expect that people are always the same and do not change much. Usually, they are most comfortable with "absolutes"; they believe in fundamentals like "good and evil," and traditions are sacrosanct. Even in the family, they are guided by imperatives—everyone is supposed to do what they are expected to do. Most of these individuals are very patriotic and see duty to others as an important goal. As consumers, they will spend money on social activities and like to buy things. It is common for people in these countries that they attribute success and failure to luck or things outside of the control of the individual. In third-world countries of this type, there is usually little or no real economic growth.

In cultures that are more long-term oriented, they usually feel like the most important things in their lives will be in the future, and people tend to adapt to changes expecting that things will get better. They are also more likely to think in terms of situational relativism—this means that they will judge a particular event or circumstance as being good or evil depending upon the situation in which it occurs. Similarly, although they may value tradition, they feel that as circumstances change, traditions should adapt as well. Family and work-team life is guided by collaboration and shared tasks, and these people are willing to learn from other countries and cultures to find the best ways to move into the future. Not surprisingly, they also tend to focus on savings and investments and are focused on doing well in the future. Students and employees in these types of cultures will look at success and failure as due to ability and effort rather than chance or luck. From a business standpoint, these cultures are usually in positions to become more prosperous in the future and to see their econo-mies grow.

Indulgent versus Restrained

This dimension is best understood as a measure of how happy people feel in a specific culture. It also has to do with the extent to which a society permits and encourages people to meet their own needs and to pursue hap-piness on their own terms as long as it does not interfere with the lives of others or is a detriment to society.

In an indulgent culture, there would be a higher percentage of people claiming that they are happy, and they would also have a perception of being able to control the important elements of their own lives. This type of culture would put a high value on freedom of speech and expression and being able to say and do what they want. They would also expect to have control over their time and to enjoy and pursue leisure activities. People in this type of culture are more likely to remember positive feelings and events in their past and not to dwell on the negatives. When the citizens are well educated, one would also expect higher birth rates because they would see the positives for having children and bringing them into the world. Since people value leisure activities, there would likely be a higher percentage of people engaged in sports, but because they are more "pleas-ure oriented," there would also be a higher percentage of obese people. Particularly in more wealthy countries, you would expect more lenient sex-ual norms. In countries of this sort, the idea of maintaining order is not an important social value either.

Restrained cultures will very likely have fewer people claiming to be happy, and there will be more people feeling that their life is largely out of their control, and they feel helpless to change very much that affects them. They do not expect or value freedom of speech or expression as much, and there is less emphasis on leisure time and activities. In countries like this with an educated populace, the birth rates would be lower because people would feel that adding children to a bad situation would not be good to do. Further, they would be less likely to remember positive events and emotions, and they would be more likely to remember and dwell on the negatives. Fewer people would probably participate in sports, but in the wealthier countries of this sort, there would also probably be fewer obese people. One would expect stricter sexual norms and a greater emphasis on maintaining social control; there would be more police officers per 100,000 population than in indulgent cultures.

Some Cultural Differences on Hofstede's Dimensions

Cultures with high power distance are more aware of differences between people of different social and economic status. In organizations, they tend to see the people in higher positions as very different from people in lower positions and feel that it is normal for these people to have different rights and privileges. Cultures with high power distance scores include those from Latin American, Asian, African, Southern and Eastern European, and Arab countries. Conversely, lower power distance scores tend to be found in Northern European countries, Israel, and Great Britain.

Regarding individualism, there is a gap between Western countries and Eastern countries. North America and Europe tend to be individualistic, whereas cultures in Asia, Africa, and Latin America tend to be much more collectivist. Interestingly, Japan and the Arab world are more in the middle on this dimension. With respect to work values, those from individualistic cultures would tend to work for personal reasons and feel that they should take care of themselves and their families first. Workers in more collectivist cultures usually feel that working is something that they do for the general good of society and that the main reason for working is to do their duty for the country and for others.

Uncertainty avoidance scores are highest in the Latin American countries, Southern and Eastern European countries, including German-speaking countries, and Japan. Countries that are less risk-avoidant and have low uncertainty avoidance scores are found in Anglo (Great Britain, United States, Canada, Australia, and New Zealand), Nordic (Scandinavian), and Chinese cultures. As one might expect, things like pensions and job security are much more important in countries that are higher in uncertainty avoidance, and in countries with lower uncertainty avoidance, workers are more likely to take risks, change jobs, try to start their own business, and be more oriented toward short-term gains.

With respect to Masculinity–Femininity, the Nordic countries are the lowest in Masculinity, while it is very high in Japan and in European countries like Hungary, Austria, and Switzerland—those influenced by

German culture. In the Anglo world, Masculinity is usually high, with the United Kingdom being one of the highest. Interestingly, in the Latin American cultures, there is quite a bit of spread on this dimension; for example, Venezuela is high on Masculinity whereas Chile is very low. With respect to how this variable impacts the workplace, one would expect that there would be stereotypical career selection with men taking traditional male jobs and women choosing those types of jobs where they would be expected to demonstrate more masculine traits and to be more aggressive than most women. It would also be expected that men would more frequently be in positions of authority and decision making and women would be more likely to be in more subservient positions.

Long-term orientation is typically found in East Asia with countries like China, Japan, and Hong Kong scoring very high on this dimension. In Eastern and Western Europe, the cultures seem to be more in the middle range on this dimension, while the Anglo cultures, the Muslim world, Africa, and Latin America are usually very short-term oriented; in fact, the United States is one of the most short-term oriented of the countries studied. Interestingly, most of the countries that are short-term oriented are in some of the emerging economies, and this makes sense because they would want to make quick progress to try to catch up with the more economically dominant countries. However, the United States has a strong economy but is very short-term oriented; in fact, this may be in part as to why the United States is not as economically dominant as it used to be and is falling behind some other countries with even stronger economies.

Because the newest dimension, Indulgence versus Restrained, is so recently described, there is less research and data on it. However, what we do have suggests that Indulgence is highest in Latin America, parts of Africa, the Anglo world, and Nordic Europe. Restraint is more frequently found in East Asia, Eastern Europe, and the Muslim world.

APPLICATIONS OF KNOWLEDGE OF CULTURAL DIFFERENCES IN WORK

It should be obvious that different countries will have cultures that differ from one another. In the past, it may not have made much difference in day-to-day work lives, but in the world today, we often must deal with people from different cultures almost daily. For example, we go to the corner store and find that the clerk appears to be from another country and we are not sure exactly how we should talk to them without being rude. Or we call a technical helpline for one of our electronic gadgets and have trouble understanding the technical support person because he or she speaks with an accent. We might even be in a situation where we have to travel to another country on behalf of our company to take care of some business issues where we need to deal with people from a different culture who may speak another language besides English.

The world of business is global today, and most organizations need to deal with people and companies from many different parts of the world. When we travel overseas, it becomes very apparent that other countries work differently than we are used to, and sometimes it is difficult to know exactly how we should deal with them. There are several areas where our knowledge of other countries can be very helpful in business and in the world of work.

Communication

Probably the most obvious area where cultural differences are a factor is communication. Of course, if people are speaking a different language, that will be an obvious problem unless they also speak English, we can also speak their language, or we may have to have a translator. In most well-educated and industrialized countries, many, if not most, of the population are multilingual, but that does not mean that they will all speak our language, so that is an issue we must address immediately or communication will be difficult. If we can get past the language barrier, however, there are still many areas where communication will be confusing. It is very important to be aware of some of the subtle communication and social issues, because something that might be normal on one culture could be a real problem in another. For example, in North America, it is expected that when you are communicating with someone, you should make eye contact; in fact, people will often not trust someone who does not keep eye contact during communication because it is assumed that he or she is not being honest. However, in other cultures, it is considered very rude for a person of lower status to make eye contact with a person of higher status. There are some cultures where a man making eye contact with a woman who is not his wife, daughter, or relative is very inappropriate and would be looked at very negatively; the same concerns also relate to things like gestures, postures, tone of voice, and other things.

Cultures also differ in how they address one another, give gifts, have meals together, spend time together, how familiar or friendly they are with one another, and how much personal information they share. Even the way people dress, how punctual they are, if they shake hands or bow, or even if they speak first or wait to be spoken to will make a difference in some cultures. When companies send employees or managers to conduct business or even work in another culture, they need to do several things if they want the person to be successful. First, they need to select people who have an interest and ability to work with different types of people in different cultures. Second, they need to provide thorough training to help the person understand the language, culture, and social practices in the new culture. If these steps are not taken, it is very unlikely that the employee or manager will be very effective or accomplish the goals of their mission. When dealing with other cultures, the most important thing to deal with is communication.

Negotiation

There are many differences in cultures with respect to issues involving negotiation. For example, in some cultures, bargaining and negotiation are simply part of doing business, whereas in others, overt bargaining and negotiation may be perceived as rude, and issues must be resolved in subtler and less direct ways. However, there are many other ways in which cultural differences will impact negotiation. For example, things like communication style, social expectations, and types and importance of various issues and goals will be influenced by the cultures involved and how they see these topics. One would expect that if the parties involved in negotiations would consider the cultural differences and negotiate accordingly, the outcomes would be better and less complicated and would reduce frustration and conflicts.

One example of how cultural differences would affect negotiation would be a situation among Canadian or American parties negotiating with Chinese executives. The North Americans would want to discuss the relevant issues, reach an agreement, sign the contract, and leave. On the other hand, the Chinese would want to spend time in nonbusiness activities, small talk, and hospitality with preferences for protocol and form and to develop a trusting relationship before entering the actual discussion of the issues. From the perspective of the North Americans, all of this "extra stuff" is just wasting time and not getting business taken care of. However, from the point of the Chinese, they cannot imagine trying to do important business with people whom you do not know very well.

Another example of how negotiating between different cultures can be somewhat confusing would involve Western business people negotiating with their counterparts in a Middle Eastern country. In Western countries, negotiation should lead to mutual understanding and agreement and then to "shake hands" to signify that the agreement has been reached, and now it is time to start working together. However, in the Middle Eastern country, much more negotiation must take place leading into an "agreement," and the handshake does not mean that an agreement has been reached; rather, it shows that the serious negotiation is ready to begin.

International Management

International management can refer to a number of things: managing people from different parts of the world; managing in a culture other than your own; managing a task force or group that has members from different countries; working for a company that is based in another country but you are still working in your country; and, working for a company from a different country and working in that (or another) foreign country. In today's global work environment, these possibilities exist in many settings and for many different employees and managers.

To help people work or manage cross-culturally, companies should provide some training to help people work and manage more effectively. The first type of training is to educate people about the nature of the culture in which they will be working or where their employees or customers are coming from. Just being aware of the cultural differences and some of the important considerations to keep in mind when dealing with people from these different cultures is a good first step, but it is not enough. In addition to cultural awareness, employees and managers need to know how to function in these different situations and how to handle some of the issues that will likely arise. Thus, we must know *about* cultural differences, but we also need to know *what we need to do to manage them*. More companies are doing a better job of training people in cultural awareness, but many do little more than that. The same kinds of work patterns that will make someone successful in one culture may be an impediment in another. Even how a manager rewards or recognizing worker's performance needs to keep in mind the cultural background of the employee. For example, a good way to motivate many workers from Western countries is to publicly recognize and praise them; however, if the employee is from a collectivist background (e.g., China, Vietnam, Korea), singling an individual out and recognizing him or her in front of his or her colleagues is likely to be embarrassing and humiliating to the employee.

As you might expect, marketing products or services in different countries is also something that must be done sensitively. For example, if you are trying to sell cars in a society where uncertainty avoidance is high, one would probably want to emphasize the safety and reliability of the cars. However, in other countries, you might want to emphasize social image and prestige. Even marketing cell phones would need to be different depending on the country in which you are trying to sell them. If you are selling phones in a collectivist country like China, you would want to emphasize the collective experience and how the cell phones help a person be a productive member of society and support the collective social good. However, if selling phones in the United States, it would be better to stress how important the cell phone would be for an individual to manage his or her time and finances more effectively.

The important thing to remember about international management is that in the global business environment of today, it is no longer possible to stick to one way of doing things, just because that is the way it has always been done. To survive and hopefully succeed in business today, companies, managers, and workers need to be aware, educated, flexible, and adaptable to all the complexity the new global environment brings. However, it is also important to remember that with these complications, there are also many new opportunities that were never available to us before, and we should try to do all that we can to take advantage of them.

OTHER DIFFERENCES BETWEEN COUNTRIES AND CULTURES

Cultural differences can affect many (probably all or most) elements of the work environment, and being aware of the dominant culture will determine many aspects of the workplace, including how it is designed. For example, in cultures that are very aware of hierarchical differences, one would expect that the design of collaborative space would be different in high-versus low-power distance cultures. In countries like the Netherlands, which is very low in power distance and thus not very hierarchical, it would be expected that collaboration would include employees and managers, and therefore the collaborative spaces would be readily accessible and even near the entrance of the building, which would encourage people from all parts of the organization to get involved with collaborative efforts frequently and easily. However, in other countries like Russia, they are much more hierarchical and very aware of status differences. Therefore, collaborative spaces would not be near where the managers are, which would imply that the upper echelon of management would be "above" the usual collaborative endeavors of the common working person. Similarly, in very masculine cultures like Germany, they tend to be much more competitive, and in this type of culture, collaborative spaces should be placed near "crossroads" where people would see one another frequently and see the benefit to working together to accomplish their goals more effectively.

CULTURAL EXPECTATIONS REGARDING HOW MUCH INDIVIDUALS WORK

There are many different reasons why people choose to work, and as we discussed earlier in this book, how much people work depends on why they are working and what their goals are. However, it is also true that some cultures have very different ideas about how many hours a day or how many weeks per year any individual employee should spend working. Obviously, if one is living in a subsistence economy where people's day-to-day survival depends on working to secure food, then they will work as much as they must, and there will not be much distinction between work and nonwork time—people will usually work most of their waking hours. However, there are some countries (mostly in Western Europe) where people expect six to eight weeks of vacation per year and never work more than 35 hours per week. There are some very interesting differences in work time and work-life balance around the world, and we will explore some of the recent research on these issues.

On a list of 35 countries in the Organization for Economic Cooperation and Development (OECD), the average number of hours worked per year is 1,766 hours, whereas workers in Mexico work the most hours and those in Germany work the least. Of these countries, the U.S. workers work more than most countries (1,790 hrs.), and there are only 12 countries that report workers putting in more time at work than U.S. employees, and there are 24 countries (mostly Western Europe, but other countries as well) that work less than the United States. Even Japanese workers, who have been known to work far more than most other employees, work less than American workers. The top five countries in terms of the most hours worked per year are Mexico (2,246 hrs.), South Korea (2,113 hrs.), Greece (2,042 hrs.), Chile (1,988 hrs.), and Poland (1,963 hrs.). At the other end of the spectrum are the five countries where workers work the fewest number of hours per year: Germany (1,371 hrs.), the Netherlands (1,419 hrs.), Norway (1,424 hrs.), Denmark (1,457 hrs.), and France (1,482 hrs.). Many countries are concerned about the amount of time people are working and are trying to do something about that. For example, in South Korea, the government has begun experimenting with the idea of putting a maximum number of hours per week that employees can be required to work, although they do allow for overtime if needed.

Japan has also begun taking overwork very seriously and largely because of some of the negative events that have occurred in that country. The Japanese identified a condition called "karōshi," which is death from overwork—usually because of a stroke or heart attack. The first official case of this problem was identified in 1969 and became an official condition in 1978. The Japanese government, businesses, and employees have started trying to do more to limit overwork and to reduce some of the problems associated with the unreasonable number of hours people were working. In other countries like the United States, we refer to "workaholism," and this has been taken to mean that some people have a trait that makes them want or need to work more than they really have to. Some research has found that "workaholism" is more often the result of demands from work than people's traits, but we do know that some people, for example, baby boomers, seem to feel a sense of pride about working hard and doing more than is required. Thus, overworking might be a result of people's traits or preferences but very frequently appears to be people responding to demands in their jobs.

Overworking has many negative outcomes that create considerable problems for individual workers, families, and society. People who work excessive hours have more health problems, are less involved with and committed to their families (although they usually think that overwork means that they are *more* committed to their families), are less efficient in their work, have lower job satisfaction, are less productive, and are more likely to leave a job if they get another offer.

Americans should be concerned about the number of hours that we work; most of the rest of the world thinks that we work unreasonable hours, and we do not seem to feel that there is anything wrong with that. In fact, in this country it is often seen as an issue of freedom—employees are free to work for any company that they want and employers are free to require people to work as many hours as are needed; that is, if they want to keep their job. In 1960 only 20 percent of mothers worked, but today over 70 percent of children live in families where all the adults in the home have jobs outside of the home. The United States is the *only* country in the Americas (North and South) without a paid parental leave benefit (taking time off to take care of child if they are ill, having problems at school, etc.). The average is over 12 weeks except in Europe where over 20 weeks of paid parental leave is usually available. In fact, in all industrialized countries, the United States is the *only* country without paid parental leave. Some other facts about American work hours are as follow:

- At least 134 countries have laws setting the maximum length of the work week—the United States does not.
- In the United States, over 85.8 percent of males and 66.5 percent of females work more than 40 hours per week.
- According to the International Labor Organization (ILO), Americans work 137 more hours each year than the Japanese, 260 more than British workers, and 499 than workers in France.

Some interesting findings regarding American paid vacation and sick time are as follow:

- There is no federal law in the United States requiring paid sick leave—it is in most industrialized countries.
- The United States is the only industrialized country in the world that has no legally mandated annual leave.
- In every one of the OECD countries except Japan and Canada (and the United States, which averages 13 days/year of paid vacation time), workers in general get 20 days of vacation time per year, and France and Finland get 30 days/year.

Why is the United States so backward when it comes to worker benefits and particularly when we see how badly we measure up to the rest of the world? The problem is probably because politicians need money to run their campaigns, and much of that funding comes from large donors and corporations that would rather not see these kinds of laws passed. It is also true that our government has made it very difficult for unions to have much influence in the workplace, and so any realistic opportunity for collective bargaining is not very likely. Thus, paying for political influence and limiting the effectiveness of unions have kept the United States behind most of the rest of the world in terms of protecting workers from abuse and overwork.

SOME CHANGES IN EXPECTATIONS OF WORKERS TODAY

One major change in the work environment today involves the increased need for workers to be more flexible and adaptive to changes. Some cultures encourage workers to be mobile and to get around the organization and see and work with people from different areas. In addition to providing collaborative spaces, these types of cultures would also provide "nomadic spaces" where people can wander around and easily interact with others. Although this would not work very well in all cultures, it does seem to be positively valued in countries like Germany, the Netherlands, and the United States, where mobility and flexibility are very good things.

One of the areas regarding cultural differences that frequently leads to misunderstandings and hurt feelings is social interactions. All cultures have guidelines or "norms" that indicate how people interact with one another in various situations, and when these norms are violated, this may result in awkward or sometimes difficult situations. For example, in China, Saudi Arabia, or Brazil, interpersonal trust results from people interacting closely over time. That is, to trust someone, you must spend time with the person and get to know him or her, and after the trust is established, you can start working together productively. Conversely, in the United States, Denmark, or the Netherlands, trust is developed by working together on business activities; therefore, you work together first and then trust develops. Clearly, one must be aware of these differences when trying to work with people from other cultures.

Another area where cultural differences can be an issue is respect for the issues of harmony and control in business activities. Americans emphasize control and mastery, whereas the Chinese are most concerned with maintaining balance and making sure that the overall system is in harmony. For example, in meetings, Americans expect to make decisions and getting things done, identify the problem, put all the ideas on the table, discuss all the options, and decide. People are expected to participate, and to not contribute is a negative thing, and if you disagree publicly with your boss and you are correct, then you are perceived to have courage and intelligence for standing up for what you think is right. However, in Asia, meetings are very different. Commonly, everyone already knows about all the issues and the decisions that have already been made; meetings are not intended to be for further discussion or debate, and disagreeing with a senior person would be perceived as very inappropriate. In these types of cultures, meetings are intended to help the group attain harmony, which is the principle goal for the group in question.

In today's world of business, most cultures will use teams in the work setting. Although this is very common, the meaning and function of a team would be very different in a highly collective culture like India or China; teams' roles are shared and fluid with people supporting one another and pitching in when extra help is needed. In this type of culture, the rewards and recognition are preferred to be shared, and employees would be very uncomfortable being singled out for special contributions or considerations. In highly individualistic cultures like the United States, Canada, and Australia, teams are still widely used, but workers and managers will look at them differently. Each team member will see themselves and one another as individuals working together for a common purpose but still expect to be seen and recognized for their individual contributions. In this type of culture, it would not be uncommon for workers to expect that in addition to the rewards and recognition given to and shared by all of the team, they would also expect to be recognized and rewarded for their individual contributions. They may understand the importance and reasons for using teams, but it will mean something very different to them than for workers and managers in more collectivist countries.

It is more common around the world to have countries that are "mixed" with respect to the individuality/collectivist dimension and thus would have some characteristics of both and be in the middle of many of these types of issues. Countries like Germany, Russia, and Brazil are more "mixed," and although they work together in teams, they prefer clearly defined roles and identifiable contributions. They may be open to 360° feedback (from superiors, subordinates, and peers) and see this as a way of helping each other and the team while still considering individual performance. Thus, the team goals and outcomes are shared and supported, but they want to keep some way to recognize and consider individual performance as well.

Some cultures are very mindful of status differences, and social and work hierarchies are seen as being very important. Traditionally, in Britain, there was a nobility as well as landed gentry and people with titles who were perceived to be different (better?) than everyone else. This was a very hierarchical culture at that time, but in the more recent history, this may be part of the culture, but it is not looked at in the same way at all. Interestingly, in Germany, titles are very important, but there is an important difference in the meaning of titles in Germany compared to many other countries. For many, probably most, cultures, titles imply status that is given to someone because of his or her position; in Germany, the title implies expertise rather than status, and thus people are respected because of the expertise that the title implies rather than just the title itself. This leads to some interesting outcomes when managers come into Germany expecting that their title and position should give them a certain degree of respect, but from the German workers and managers, the respect has to be earned by establishing expertise first.

There are also differences between countries with respect to relatively how much time is spent on analysis before one acts. Obviously, all managers and business people will analyze a situation or problem before they act, but this is handled very differently in different countries. Many global businesses (especially westerners) will be frustrated when working with companies in Russia, India, or Brazil when projections or reports are late or other time commitments are not complied with. Some may see this as laziness, but it really is an indication of how they approach decision making and action. In countries like Russia, India, and Brazil, they are less interested in deadlines than they are in fully understanding the situation and all the dynamics; for these countries, analysis and understanding are more important than timelines. However, for North Americans and Western Europeans, timelines and deadlines are obligations within which the company is expected to comply. This is clearly not a "right-wrong" type of situation, although either party may feel that way. However, when working with organizations from different cultures, one must be prepared to work with people whose views, goals, and perspectives may not be the same as ours, and this means that we must try to understand, accommodate, compromise, collaborate, and yet be appropriately assertive about the things that are truly important to us, if we are to be able to productively work with and enjoy people from other cultures.

Interestingly, Switzerland is a country where they seem to be in the middle of most of the cultural dimensions that we examine. They try to have a balanced perspective on all the important cultural questions, and this is probably for a variety of reasons. Although it is a small country, there are distinctly different parts of the country that were fairly independent of one another because of the mountains separating them. In fact, while German is the official language of Switzerland, there are regions where other languages are spoken as well, including Schweizerdeutsch (Swiss German), which is a little different from High German, and it is only spoken—there is no written Schweizerdeutsch. Other parts of Switzerland speak French, Italian, and Romanisch (an old version of Latin, spoken by the Romans who occupied parts of Switzerland in the past). In addition to being culturally diverse, Switzerland is geographically small, which means that most people have learned to understand and get along with people who are physically close to them but may be somewhat different culturally. The Swiss are politically neutral and proud of it, but they are also rather culturally neutral. Because of their history of neutrality, this may be one of the reasons why they are bankers for much of the rest of the world, and their very friendly tax advantages make it attractive to many world businesses to locate there. Although there are benefits to having a balanced perspective like the Swiss, that does not mean that it is the best way to be, and this approach would not work in many other countries. However, it does mean that the Swiss often enjoy and deal very well with people from many different cultures.

SUMMARY AND CONCLUSION

By examining the role and importance of culture when trying to understand the psychology of work, it gets complicated very quickly. For example, it is tempting to act as if all the people in each culture share the same values and cultural attributes, and of course, this is never true. National culture has a significant effect of the thoughts, feelings, and actions of everyone in the culture, but that does not mean that everyone will act, think, or feel the same ways. Every person will have a different personality, a different history, and different factors influencing them. Similarly, every organization will have a dominant culture, and although that may significantly influence people in the organization, it is also true that various people in the organization will still be different from one another in many ways. If these things are so variable and can differ so much, why even bother trying to study them? If we know, in general, how many or most people in each culture are going to perceive or act in certain situations, it will significantly help us to understand them and to avoid the kinds of misunderstandings that make it difficult to work together productively or to interact in ways that will help accomplish the goals of all the people involved.

The fact that culture adds many layers of complexity to the understanding of human behavior in the workplace does not mean that we should ignore it because it is so complicated. The more we learn about cultural differences and how they impact people and the workplace, the more likely we are to be able to work more effectively with other people and to help organizations and employees accomplish their goals efficiently and productively. The world is getting smaller very quickly, and being able to deal with people and organizations from many different parts of the world is more important than it has ever been. Even travel to other countries has become so much easier and more common that to encounter and enjoy other cultures is more in the reach of many people than ever before.

In the past, many Americans expected to travel to other countries and have everyone they needed to deal with understand English; some would even be annoyed with people who did not speak American English. "If they want our money, they should learn our language" was the way that some people felt. Today, most of the educated world is multilingual, and they expect to deal with people from other areas of the globe, but most Americans are still very much monolingual. As we are dealing more with the rest of the world in business, we are finding it increasingly more important to be culturally sensitive, well informed, and educated in other languages. Some companies, especially in California and the Southwest, will hire many seasonal workers from Latin American countries. Unlike the political fear mongering that we have heard in recent years, most of the workers who come north of the border to work are perfectly legal and documented. Many of these companies will provide free classes for English as a second language; the idea is that they want the employees to be as effective as they can be, and understanding English will make them better employees. Interestingly, some of these companies also provide Spanish language courses for English-speaking managers and employees. The rationale is that the better the employees and managers communicate, the more effectively the work will be performed. Although some would see this as taking jobs away from American residents, the reality is that these companies cannot hire enough resident Americans to fill the jobs, and without the seasonal employees coming north for jobs, the cost of food and other products would be far higher than they already are. This is an example of a situation where workers and managers may be from very different cultures and speak different languages, but by working together and learning from one another, the jobs get done better and faster, and the company accomplishes its goals more effectively and completely. Learning about, understanding, and appreciating cultural difference will make workers and organizations more effective and more positive.

Part II

Scenarios

In this section of the book, we will present various "real-life" scenarios that involve people at work and will address different types of situations that people might encounter at work. As you read them, it will be interesting to see how you think that these situations might be resolved. In these examples, we will analyze them and make suggestions as to how they might be resolved, and it will be interesting to see how your ideas about these situations will be similar or different from the ones we suggest. Of course, there are no right or wrong answers, and every situation and person is unique. One thing that you may discover is that to handle situations appropriately, you may need to consider many different issues and points of view.

 Staying Motivated

Amy is a 20-year-old young woman who is going to college and living with two friends in an apartment. To support herself she has taken out college loans, but she is also working part-time at a doughnut shop for minimum wage. She really needs the job, and it is in a convenient location that is easy for her to get to, and it is close to her apartment and school. Her boss is OK and is very flexible with her hours and will work with her college schedule. Although there are things that make this a good job for her, she does not like working in the doughnut shop because she is trying to lose weight and hates being tempted by the Boston

Creams every day. She also does not have much in common with her coworkers, and although most of them are not too difficult to deal with, there are a few who are obnoxious, and one guy keeps "hitting on her" and simply will not take "No" for an answer. This is not a job that she wants to keep any longer than she must, is not interested in getting more hours than she is currently receiving, and is not concerned about a promotion—she just wants to do her job, get her paycheck, and leave.

She is living in the same town she grew up in, and her parents and brother also live locally. Although she does not have a regular boyfriend, she does date occasionally, and there are a couple of guys whom she might get interested in. She visits her family once a week or so to do her laundry and to get some "home cooking," which is a nice treat. She gets along fine with her family, but they are not financially able to help her with college other than feeding her occasionally.

The main problem that she has at work is motivation—the job is not terrible, her coworkers are all right (mostly), and her boss is OK. However, she dreads going to work, does a good job, but never goes out of her way to do more than she absolutely must. Some people might think that she is lazy, but that is not true; she just does not really care about the job or the people at work. The real question for Amy is, "What can she do to get a little more motivated for work and to possibly enjoy it more?"

Motivation is a bit of a tricky issue from a psychological perspective. We never actually see motivation directly but infer it from looking at changes in behavior. If we give someone positive feedback about his or her job performance and then notice that he or she is working harder, we might very appropriately assume that the positive feedback increased the worker's motivation.

For Amy to be more motivated in her current job situation, we should break it down into what it is that Amy wants to be different. To begin with, she would like to enjoy the job more—that is, to have higher job satisfaction. Further, she would probably like to enjoy her coworkers more than she does and would like to avoid being tempted by the doughnuts that she really does not feel like she should eat. Of course, she would like to earn more money but is not interested, nor does she have the time in working more hours or taking on more responsibilities. By looking at motivation from the standpoint of goals or objectives in this situation, it will be easier to suggest and implement changes in Amy's behavior that might help her attain the outcomes she wants at work or at least to minimize the things that she dislikes.

To help Amy enjoy what she is doing at work, we need to remind her why she is working. This job is not a career, nor is it something that she intends to continue after she leaves this job. She took this job because she needed to make money to help support herself while she is in college. Second, the job is conveniently located, so it does not take more time to get to work, and it does not require her to use much gas for her car or to spend money on a bus. Third, her boss is very flexible about her hours and is good about letting her work her hours around her college schedule. Fourth, most of her coworkers are decent people who are nice to her. Finally, even though this is not a great job, by doing her work conscientiously, she will have an opportunity for a good reference for future jobs, and it does look good to employers that she worked during college, managed her time well, and supported herself—even in this type of job. To get herself more motivated, one thing that Amy needs to do is to remind herself that this job is meeting her needs and goals very well now; this job is not a career—it is a paycheck and a temporary solution to some very specific but important short-term needs.

One specific thing that she can do to improve her motivation and job satisfaction is to change her own behavior in the situations that bother her. We can never improve things for ourselves by waiting around for other people to change—if we want things to be different for ourselves, we need to look at what is under our control and what we can do differently. For example, if she wants to enjoy the people at work, she can talk to them more, get to know them better, and ask about their lives and interests. Even the guy who is "hitting on her" could possibly be dealt with differently. She could tell him that she really is not interested in going out, and she would appreciate it if he would not keep asking her. If he does not respect that request, then I would ask for a meeting with the boss and with this worker, and she could say that she is not interested in getting him in trouble but really would like him to stop asking her for a date and flirting with her. The boss can handle this in a way that is not threatening but just reinforces the idea that sexual harassment is not acceptable in the workplace. To keep from being tempted by the doughnuts, she can substitute something whenever she has the urge of having one. She can get something else that is nonfattening, she can go talk to a coworker to get her mind off the doughnuts, or she can even ask the boss if there is some other task or chore she can do.

By addressing her own needs and goals is one way that she can foster better work motivation, and by addressing directly some of the things that she does not like about work will help. The main thing to remember is that the best chance she has of making things better is to look at changes she is willing and able to make herself.

Clashing with a Boss

Tom has a good job working as a teller at a bank. Although it is not a great paying job, he feels that there are opportunities for him to move up the ladder and get into a management position. He is a college graduate and thinks that he would be a good candidate for promotion when an opportunity arises. He also likes working in a bank and feels that this bank is one that he would enjoy making a career in. However, for all the things that he likes about the job and the bank, there is one thing that is a real problem—his boss. The head teller is demanding and insulting, never has a good thing to say, is never complementary, and never seems to be helpful to any of his subordinates. Tom recognizes that his boss treats others just as badly as he treats Tom, so he concluded that it is not him but is obviously the boss who is the problem in this situation. Other than leaving the job, which he does not want to do, he is not sure how he can make this situation better.

He is presently living with his parents and younger sister who is going to the local community college, and he hopes to save enough money to be able to move out and get his own place. He does have a regular girlfriend who lives locally with her parents, and they plan to get engaged soon (when he can afford to buy a ring); further, they plan to get married in a couple of years. It seems that he is doing all the right and responsible things both personally and professionally, but he wishes that things could move along quicker. Although he does not particularly like his present job because of his boss, he hesitates leaving because he knows that he will start back at the bottom wherever he goes, and since he likes banking, he feels that he is better off just staying where he is. However, he finds that the longer he is in the job, the more annoying his boss becomes, and as Tom gets more experience and learns more, he feels that his manager is finding him a little threatening, and particularly because many of the other tellers come to Tom for advice rather than going to the head teller.

Tom has tried to talk to the head teller about some of his concerns but finds that when he asks for help or clarification or tries to explain himself, his boss just lashes out at him and blames him for even more problems. As critical as his boss is, however, Tom must admit that even though his annual reviews are not "glowing," they are at least moderately positive. He has considered going to the head teller's boss but fears that might make the situation even worse, and he also does not like being perceived by management as a "tattler" or "whiner." He is at a loss as to what to do because he does not like the present situation but feels that leaving the job would be a mistake.

Tom's dilemma is that he likes and wants his job, likes the organization, but has difficulty getting along with his boss. This is one of those situations where you must look at the rewards and costs of staying or leaving and to understand what is under your control and what is not. The best solution would be if Tom's boss suddenly decided that he was being a jerk and became a nicer person—not a likely event. The way Tom seems to feel now is that the rewards of staying seem to outweigh the costs (dealing with his boss), and the costs of leaving (giving up a job he likes in a company and industry he hopes to have a future in) appear to outweigh the rewards of leaving (being away from the boss and *maybe* finding another good job that he likes). Thus, if he stays, then he must accept the cost, which is remaining with the same boss.

Now Tom needs to examine what things are under his control and what things are not. Clearly, he has no control over his boss's behavior, and although he could go over his boss's head and complain to upper management, the risk of doing that probably outweighs the possible benefit. When there is a conflict between an employee and a manager, the organization will rarely fire the manager and keep the lower-level employee, unless, of course, there is a situation involving discrimination or harassment. The only real control Tom has in this situation is his own behavior and actions; thus, any changes in the situation will need to come from him.

Tom will probably try to remain in the situation and find better ways to deal with his boss. He should not approach the situation trying to figure out what he can do to make his boss change—he probably is not going to change very much. However, Tom can probably find ways to deal with him that at least makes Tom feel better. When people are in situations where they feel trapped, one important thing to do is to try to find anything in the situation that they can change that is under their control—even if it is just a tiny thing. For example, when other employees are complaining about the boss, Tom should keep quiet and not say anything; in fact, he would be better off just excusing himself and getting back to work—the more he talks about how miserable this person is, the worse he will feel about it. He can also maintain his distance; he should be courteous and respectful but should not go out of his way to be friendly—just be professional. If his boss is critical, he should listen and ask if his boss has any suggestions as to how he might do his job better. If his boss gives him an order or suggestion that Tom does not agree with, he should respectfully suggest that he might try something a little differently and give some reasons why. If his boss insists that Tom follows his directions, he should just agree and go ahead as directed and do as good a job as he can—after all, he is the boss. By doing his job well, maintaining his distance, being professional and courteous, and not causing any difficulties, Tom's boss may not change, but Tom will probably feel better about his situation and it will not be so difficult.

Too Old for the Job?

Shirley is a 60-year-old woman who has worked for an insurance company for 15 years and is a secretary who serves three salespeople and does all their typing and much of the filing and helps manage their schedules. She is married with three children, and her husband has been retired from a large manufacturing company where he was a machinist. He is in generally good health and is collecting Social Security and a pension. They are not wealthy, but they are paying their bills and living comfortably. They have two adult sons and one adult daughter, all of whom live within an hour's drive. Shirley feels that she cannot retire until she reaches 65 because they still need the income and until she qualifies for Social Security and can get her own pension, she cannot afford to quit.

In the past few years, she has noticed that some of her coworkers and superiors seem to be acting like they do not think she is "up to her job" any longer. They will sometimes give work to other secretaries and tell Shirley that they know she's busy and they do not want to burden her, and this happens even when she is not busy. They often do not give her work that requires computer skills because they seem to think that she is not good with computers even though she feels that she does have good technical skills. Her boss has been nice to her but has even said that they may be restructuring some of the work in the office because he feels that some of the things that she is asked to do is more than she is trained to do, and some of the younger people might do it more easily. Although no one has said anything about her retiring, she feels that they are just waiting for her to leave so they can bring in someone else.

The people at work, including her boss, are pleasant to her, and no one has made bad comments to her, but she has the sense that perhaps she is not valued as much as she feels that she should be. She has worked for this company for 15 years, always gotten good reviews, gets regular raises, and has never gotten negative feedback about her performance. She would like to work for a few more years, but she would also like to feel better about her job and her role in the organization. Trying to find another job at her age would be difficult, and she does not want to have to learn a new job, fit into a new company, and meet all new colleagues and managers. Now she just needs to figure out what she can do to make the last few years of her career as good as they can be.

It is certainly common for generational differences to present issues in the workplace. One increasingly common problem is for older workers to find that their supervisors and managers are about the same age as their children, and thus, the supervisors and managers are trying to find ways to manage someone who is the same generation as their parents—this can be awkward. It is particularly difficult in this type of situation when the older worker knows much more about the job and about the organization than the manager does, but the manager just assumes that the worker does not really know what he or she is talking about because he or she is old.

One thing that it is difficult for younger workers and managers to grasp is that older workers are often much more knowledgeable and even more productive than younger workers because they have more experience and they are more efficient—they may not work harder, but they do work smarter. Too often, coworkers and supervisors assume that since older workers are not as energetic, they are not as productive, but most research evidence contradicts these misconceptions. Most studies find that older workers are almost always more productive than younger workers in most jobs, but that is not the common perception.

Many times, the difficulty that an older person has is because the culture of the organization is not as comfortable for him or her because the culture may reflect the changing organization, the management, and the workplace. Often the key is for the older worker to find ways to fit into the culture more comfortably without feeling that he or she must change who he or she is or that he or she must pretend to be something that he or she is not.

Shirley cannot hope that somehow everyone else in the organization will change and be more supportive and accepting of her. It sounds like people in the organization appreciate and are nice to her, but it also seems like they may not understand her strengths and contributions. There are probably many things that she can do to make the situation better for herself. First, she could sit down with her boss and say that she wants to be as productive as possible and ask for more frequent feedback so that she can continue to improve. Even if the boss agrees, it is up to Shirley to ask for feedback when she feels that she needs some input. She can also say that she is anxious to learn some new skills and ask if she can sign up for some of the training programs that are available to employees. She should also volunteer to help with other projects and to join committees or support groups in the workplace.

With respect to her relationship to coworkers, she should not avoid them; she can sit with them in the lunch or break rooms, talk to them, ask questions about their families and activities, and just generally show interest in them as people. It is also good for her to share some of her life with the others, bring in pictures of children and grandchildren, tell about trips and vacations, and just relate comfortably with them about things other than work. It would also be good to volunteer to help coworkers when they seem overloaded or stressed; helping people just to be helpful is almost always appreciated.

It is not necessary for Shirley to feel like she must become a new person, but rather she does need to take some initiative to make the workplace more comfortable for herself. A good way for her to think about this would be to say to herself, "If I were truly comfortable here and with these people, what would I like to do in this situation?" This little guideline would probably help her feel more comfortable doing things that will be good for her and make her more a part of the culture of her work group and the organization.

 ### Starting a Business

Bill is a 45-year-old computer technician who has worked for a large retail company that sells and services computers and other electronic entertainment products. He has a decent salary, good benefits, and a solid retirement program. He is single and not in a permanent relationship, although he does have a regular girlfriend with whom he has been together for five years. He lives alone with his cat, George, and a tank of fish. He does have a good social life and has friends with whom he likes to bowl and watch sports. He has recently become increasingly dissatisfied with his job and wishes that he could start his own business selling and repairing computers. He likes his job and his coworkers, and management seems very satisfied with the quality of his work; he gets excellent performance evaluations and always gets a raise. However, he does feel like this is a dead-end job, and it is unlikely that he would make it into the management ranks of this organization.

He has talked to his friends and family about the possibility of his starting a new business, and since he is the person who usually fixes the computers of "everyone," people are very enthusiastic about his prospects. However, he also knows that the prospect of starting a new company is daunting and that it is a big risk. Having your own business sounds exciting, but it is very hard work, you rarely make much money at the beginning, and you will now have many new expenses, tax problems, employee issues, product and equipment needs and issues, as well as location and building concerns. There are many concerns involved with starting a new company. How big will the company need to be? How many employees will we need? What kinds and how much insurance will we need? What are the legal issues (incorporation, liability, etc.)? How much money will it take to get started and stay afloat? These are just a few of the issues he will need to deal with before even thinking about starting a new company.

One of the main concerns that he has is that if he goes off on his own, he will lose his health insurance, a life insurance policy through his company, a regular paycheck, sick leave, and vacation time; these concerns weigh heavily on his mind. However, he also feels that if he were ever to do this, now would be the best time. He does not have a family to support, no one depends on him financially, he is in good health, and even in the worst-case scenario, even if the business fails, he can just go and get another job. He does own his own home, and it will be paid off in ten years, so he feels that if he can make enough money to support his home, car, taxes, expenses, and health care, he should be fine, but of course there is no guarantee with a new business that it will make any money, let alone a profit.

Starting a new business is a very risky enterprise, and research has shown that the very large majority of new businesses fail in the first 18 months. Most people have no idea as to what is involved with starting a new company. For example, it takes more than being a good cook to run a restaurant; similarly, it takes more than knowing how to sell and fix computers to own and run a computer store. Very frequently, new businesses fail because they are undercapitalized. This means that they do not have as much money at the beginning as they will need. Usually, people do not accurately estimate how much it costs to pay for everything necessary to start a business. Further, rarely do new businesses start making money as quickly as people think that they will. Consequently, running out of money is a very frequent problem for start-ups.

It is also a common problem that the new entity is not based on good marketing information. Targeting your key customer base, adequately advertising in the right places and often enough, and locating your business where it is convenient for customers to find and access (e.g., easy to get to and convenient places to park) are just some of the marketing issues that need to be addressed. Determining things like hours of operation, number of employees, types of employees, and range of products and services to offer are also things that need to be solved. It is tempting to try to be "all things to all people" and to offer anything people might need. However, if you cannot support the things that you try to do, you will have dissatisfied customers, which is a huge problem for a new business. Further, if you try to do too much, you will probably need more employees than you can afford, and this will create new problems as well.

The first thing that Bill needs to do is some good research. Is there a demand for the type of business he wants to start? What would be the competition and how would he compete with them? What would be the target market(s) and how would he reach them? How big would the business need to be to provide the products and services he wants to? He would

have to do some digging around and might have to hire a marketing consultant to help get this information. The next step would be to develop a
business plan, and this is a very technical process for which he would also
need another expert consultant. If he cannot afford to pay for expensive
consultants, he might visit a local university with a business school and
see if some graduate students would like to take on these projects for a
small fee or even do it as part of a class project; by using the students, he
would also get some input from their professors, which might be very helpful. After the business and marketing plans are in place, he will need to
decide what he will need in terms of space, equipment, products, and
employees as well as other start-up expenses. Then he will need to go to
a bank or other lending organizations and see what kinds of loans or other
financing options might be available to help him get started financially.
After all of this is done, if he still is willing to try it, he should be ready
to launch the business.

 ## Balancing Family and Career

*Janet is a 35-year-old woman with two sons, ages 11 and 5, and a 9-year-old
daughter. For the first time in many years, Janet will have most of her days available because all her children will be in school and even the 5-year-old is in full-
day kindergarten. She graduated from high school and has three years of college
but got married before she finished her degree; she majored in sociology and had
some thoughts about being a social worker but now is not sure if she wants to
get into that type of career while she has three young children. However, she is
thinking seriously about getting back into the workforce, at least on a part-time
basis, because she does like to be home with her children when they get out of
school, and all three of them are involved in activities and lessons, so she does
do most of the transportation.*

*Janet's husband, Kyle, is a supportive husband and father and does quite
about around the house and with the children, but he is an insurance salesman
and broker, and while he makes a good living, he rarely works less than a 50–
60-hour week. Janet probably does not have to work, but the extra money would
be nice and would probably mean that they could do a little more in the way of
trips and vacations. Kyle's job provides excellent benefits, and therefore, Janet
does not have to find a job that will have retirement and health benefits. In the
past, Janet has worked in retail sales, in restaurants as a waitress, and as a clerk
in a business office. She and Kyle even talked about her working in his office, but
they decided that would probably not be a good idea, because it increased the likelihood of bringing work home with them and feeling like they were at work all the*

time. Janet also felt that it would be nice to make new friends and to be around other people during the day.

Kyle is very supportive of the idea that Janet would like to get involved with a job and even suggested that they get someone to come in to clean the house once a week so that Janet did not have to worry about that and could focus more on her job and the children. Janet discussed these ideas with some of her friends, and while all of them thought that it sounded great, none of them had any specific ideas about available jobs other than some rather general suggestions. Having been out of the workforce for many years, she was not even sure how to start looking for a job, so she started by looking online and in the newspaper.

Managing work-life balance is a challenge for everyone; to be healthy and well-adjusted, even single, independent professionals who love their work must have some other meaningful aspects of their lives outside of work. Of course, when one adds a partner or spouse, children, and pets, that balance even becomes harder to maintain. For most people, especially women, the one thing that usually gets put at the bottom of the list is taking care of themselves and their own needs, and yet this is terribly important because unless you are taking care of yourself, it is impossible to be as good a parent, partner or spouse, friend, sibling as you would want to be. Thus, maintaining balance means taking care of yourself, your obligations, your job, and the wide variety of things that are important to you.

For most people, maintaining balance usually means making compromises and trying to find more ways to be efficient, but it is never easy. It seems that Janet has a good situation with supportive people who want to help her to work if she wants to. Even before she looks for the job, she must determine what kinds of adjustments will need to be made and how all the various responsibilities will be taken care of. After these discussions have been held, she will have a better idea as to what kinds of hours she will be able to work and how many days per week she can commit. Then, she can start looking for a job and see what might be available and interesting.

Probably the first thing that should be done is for Janet and Kyle to sit down together and see how they can arrange for the normal family responsibilities to be fulfilled. For example, shopping, housekeeping, getting children to their lessons/games/practices, grocery shopping, preparing meals, and cleaning up are just a few examples of the things they should think about. Of course, each week will be a little different, and one plan will not fit all situations, but if they have some good ideas as to how to approach the schedules, it will help. For example, they should sit down as a family at a given time each week (e.g., Sunday evening) and discuss the schedule and arrangements for the next week, including meals and activities. Then they can decide how these things can be managed. Another very good idea is to have all the children have specific chores and responsibilities that are reasonable for their ages and abilities, and a small allowance is one way of giving them more of a sense of ownership of their responsibilities. Discussions will also need to be held regarding consequences for when responsibilities are not fulfilled.

For Janet to start looking for a job, the best place to start is networking. She should send e-mails or cards to friends, family, former coworkers, local business owner that she knows, and anyone she can think of who might be able to suggest a job that they are aware of. She should let them know the kinds of jobs she might consider, the kinds of hours she will be able to work, and what her basic work and educational history has been. Personal contacts are one of the best ways to find jobs and particularly if you get these ideas from people who know you and know what your skills are. She should also have an updated résumé and provide a copy to the people she is contacting in her network. When she starts interviewing, she should be very clear as to what her expectations are and emphasize that even though she is looking for part-time jobs, she wants and expects to be an involved, serious, and committed employee who has professional aspirations and is not just looking for an extra paycheck; she wants to be taken seriously as a prospective employee.

Part III

Controversies and Debates

This part of the book will address three controversial issues in the world of work and will have essays on both sides of each issue that are written by scholars and professionals in the field. As you will see, each of these perspectives has some very good and compelling reasons supporting each position, and this will give you some indication of the importance and complexity of these matters. Although you may find that you agree with one side more than the other, it is very likely that you will at least appreciate that the other viewpoint does have some good points and that the issues are not as straightforward or simple as they might initially seem. After you have read both the positions of these three controversial issues, it will be interesting to see how you feel about them and if your perspectives have changed.

 Controversy #1: Does Setting Goals Help or Harm Workers' Performance?

INTRODUCTION

The question as to whether goal setting is helpful or problematic is not a simple one, nor is there a single, simple answer. Clearly, there are some good things about setting goals; but there are some risks as well, and there have been some lively debates in the scholarly and popular literature. It may be hard to imagine in our culture, but as logical as setting goals may sound, it is not as simple as it might seem. In this global environment, we often lose sight of the fact that other cultures may not look at things, including goal setting, the same way we do, and not all cultures would think in terms of goal setting to improve performance. For example, in some cultures, they feel that most things that occur are predestined, and people have little control over what happens to them; if you really believe that, then setting individual goals seems irrelevant. Consider as well that in a more collectivist country, work is primarily intended to support the state and society; setting individual goals would not make much sense because people are paid based upon their need rather than their performance, and it is assumed that they would work as hard as they could for the benefit of their country.

Americans, particularly, think about goals frequently, and this is very much a part of our country and culture. In business, for example, having strategic plans, mission statements, performance appraisal systems, profit sharing, employee stock options, retirement plans, and so forth are all based on goals and goal setting. Athletics, performing arts, and even academic research and teaching all encompass goal setting as part of how one approaches these areas. That does not mean that other cultures do not use goals, but how goals are set and how important they are depend on the prevailing culture of the society and the organization in which people work. It also depends on the individual and how important goals are to them personally.

As we will see in the following discussions, even in the United States, there are advantages and disadvantages of goal setting. Too often, people make the mistake of looking at issues like goal setting and try to simplify them as being either good or bad. Clearly, this is not a situation that is reduceable to a simple "good-bad" or "right-wrong" opinion. Keeping in mind that when we have a complex situation like goal setting, the challenge is to find out what aspects of goal setting are realistic and advantageous for the organization and the people involved and then find ways to implement and take advantage of these opportunities. At the same time, we must also look at the disadvantages and try to find ways to minimize or eliminate these negative factors. By implementing the positive elements and avoiding the negative aspects, there is a good chance that goal setting can have a very beneficial impact on an organization and the people within it.

In establishing good goals, there are some steps that will allow people to set goals that are beneficial. We should clarify this issue by pointing out that "good" goals are not just goals that sound good but are ones that improve performance. We cannot evaluate goals without looking at the impact that they have on important outcomes. In organizations, good goals would be ones that will improve individual and organizational performance, decrease waste, improve efficiency and effectiveness, reduce costs, improve profits, positively impact customer/client expectations, and so forth. Thus, when we are trying to set good goals, we need to clarify what the criteria are that we are trying to affect; that is, what are we trying to accomplish with our goals? When we have our criteria in mind, we can start specifying the goals we wish to attain and then setting objectives that will lead to goal attainment.

One approach to goal setting that has been widely accepted is the use of SMART goals. "SMART" is an acronym for goals that are specific, measurable, attainable, realistic, and time-based. It is difficult to accomplish a goal that is too general or ambiguous. For example, a goal like "I want to complete my report by four o'clock this afternoon" is a very specific goal, and if it is important and realistic, this should be a goal worth pursuing. However, a goal like "I want to do a better job" is so general and ambiguous that it is hard to see how that would be very helpful in guiding behavior. It is also important that goals be measurable, and although this may not appear to be very important, it is necessary. If you cannot measure a goal or its completion, then how do you know if you have achieved it? Being measurable can be very simple; for example, "Did you get the report finished by 4 p.m. or not?" This is a simple measure, but it is a measure nonetheless. Other goals might be more complex in terms of measurement, but it is important that any goal worth accomplishing must be measurable.

Goals that are most likely to positively impact performance are challenging but attainable. Goals that are too easy are not motivating, and people will not treat them very seriously. On the other hand, goals that are so difficult that they are unlikely to be achieved are more likely to lead to frustration rather than motivation. For goals to be realistic is like being attainable, but it is a little broader. Realistic goals are ones that make sense given the situation, the ability of the person trying to fulfill them, and the amount of time and support that they have. Realistic goals give a person at least a reasonable chance of being able to achieve them. Finally, good goals are time-based, and this means that goal completion has an expectation of time to completion. For example, saying that you want to finish your report by 4 p.m. is a clear and specific time element that will make it more likely that you will try to complete the goal in the time indicated in the goal statement. An important point for organizations and managers to remember is that unrealistic time demands on goals are more likely to be discouraging than motivating; when setting time aspects of goals, it is very important to be realistic about this as well.

RESPONSE 1: GOAL SETTING HELPS EMPLOYEES' PERFORMANCE

Goal setting is one strategy for improving employees' performance in the workplace. Setting goals can provide guidance and direction for employee; it will also motivate and inspire employees while helping the organization track and evaluate employees' performance. To be most helpful, goals need to be specific and challenging and are best when determined collaboratively with the supervisor and employee working together to establish the goals and objectives. This will ensure that the goals are meaningful to the employee and beneficial to the organization.

Goals Provide Guidance and Direction

Goal setting helps to keep employees focused on their tasks and helps avoid unrelated and nonproductive activities, which also saves supervision time. Setting goals facilitates planning for employees and supervisors, enables employees to monitor and evaluate their own performance and progress, and gives supervisors clear outcomes to anticipate and to track. With effective goal setting, workers will also be more able to evaluate problems and barriers that might interfere with their performance, which will enable them to act or get help and advice to deal with these challenges. When the organization shares its goals with employees, this also allows them to see how their individual goals and performance fit into the "big picture" of the organization's mission and why their performance is important to the accomplishment of that mission.

Goals Motivate and Inspire Employees

Goals can help energize employees and can motivate them to acquire new knowledge and skills needed to achieve a challenging goal. Research has demonstrated that challenging goals lead to increased effort and performance more than easier goals, but there are four conditions that must be met for goal setting to improve performance. First, the employee must have the ability to accomplish the goal; second, it is important that the employee has access to the resources he or she needs to accomplish the goal (e.g., environmental constraints must be minimal in order for the goal to be attained); third, the employee must be personally committed to reaching the goal; and finally, the employee must receive appropriate feedback on his or her progress toward the accomplishment of the goal, which will help the employee know what tasks are being completed, which are not, and which things need to be focused on next.

Goals Help Organizations Evaluate Performance

Employees need to be measured and evaluated for meaningful feedback to occur, and performance improvement and goal setting are very important in this area. Employees and their supervisors should meet to set measurable and obtainable goals and then have regular meetings where the employee can self-evaluate and the supervisor can provide feedback regarding the employee's progress. In addition, any challenges or problems can be addressed and dealt with.

Type of Goal Matters

There are different types of goals that an individual and/or an organization can establish that involve such things as behavioral, learning, and performance objectives. Behavioral goals focus on the specific behaviors that lead to a given outcome, learning goals focus on acquiring knowledge and skills, and performance goals focus on a relevant outcome. Learning goals may be primarily associated with motivation, whereas performance goals may deal more with employees' ability and skill. Thus, the same goal could be framed differently to reflect either a learning or a performance goal. For example, a learning goal could be "Search for and implement effective strategies for increasing market share," and a performance goal could be "Attain 21 percent or more of market share." In one study, individuals who were given a learning goal performed significantly better than those who were given a performance goal. It is possible that individuals take pride in mastering skills and gaining knowledge and therefore will work harder. Thus, employees, supervisors, and organizations should consider setting learning-based goals whenever possible, although it is important to remember that there may be situations where performance-based goals might be more beneficial.

Conclusion

Goal setting is imperative for increasing employee workplace performance. However, it is very important to remember that employees must have the ability to achieve the goal, receive appropriate feedback, be given a meaningful task, and have an appropriate and supportive environment for achieving their goal. In addition, learning goals tend to be more beneficial for employees' goal attainment than performance goals in many situations. Finally, goal setting can provide the employees with a sense of accomplishment each time they reach their goal, motivating them to set new, more complex goals, thus continuing to increase their workplace performance. It is expected that better goal setting will lead to higher levels of performance and job satisfaction and ultimately to improved organizational performance.

Liesl A. Nydegger, PhD, MPH

BIBLIOGRAPHY

Latham, G., Seijts, G., & Slocum, J. (2016). The goal setting and goal orientation labyrinth: Effective ways for increasing employee performance. *Organization Dynamics, 45*(4), 271–277.

Seijts, G., Latham, G. P., Tasa, K., & Latham, B. W. (2004). Goal setting and goal orientation: An integration of two different yet related literatures. *Academy of Management Journal, 47*(2), 227–239.

RESPONSE 2: THE DISADVANTAGES OF GOAL SETTING

Although it is generally thought of as a positive endeavor, goal setting has the potential to be detrimental both personally and professionally. Unfortunately, since many people (and organizations) tend to look at outcomes as dichotomies (e.g., good-bad, right-wrong, success-failure), it is easy to see how goals can be looked at simplistically so that any unmet goal is a failure regardless of the reasons why it may not have been fulfilled. Seeing unmet goals as failures makes it more likely that people will set easier goals for themselves to make sure that they can reach them, and they will find reasons or excuses why they cannot pursue more challenging goals.

New Year's resolutions are a good example of personal goals that people might set. Frequently, people will set goals for themselves like losing weight, eating healthier, or making better lifestyle choices. Although these sound like very positive things to aspire to, people often set unrealistic goals for themselves, and when they cannot fulfill them, they get discouraged, see themselves as a failure, and then give up on the goal completely. This type of situation can also occur in the workplace. For example, many companies use "stretch goals," which means that as employees start to reach a goal, the goal is changed to a more challenging outcome, and thus the person now must focus on meeting this new and more difficult goal. There are many good examples of how stretch goals can be used productively, but unfortunately many (probably most) organizations simply keep changing goals so that the employee never has the sense of having completed a goal and succeeding, which leads to frustration, discouragement, and decreased performance.

There are other aspects of goal setting that are also problematic. For example, there is research evidence that when people are given unrealistic goals and are expected to meet them without any excuse, workers will sometimes resort to unsafe, unethical, and sometimes illegal activities just to make sure that the goals are reached. Clearly, these kinds of activities will frequently put workers, their company, and customers at risk and can even lead to difficult or even tragic outcomes. Further, people sometimes get so concerned and committed to a goal that they lose sight of the purpose of the goal and the mission of the organization. For example, if someone is told to increase his or her productivity by 20 percent by the next quarter and the person is trying to accomplish that but is not producing his or her usual quality, and he or she has been neglecting customer needs just to keep up his or her progress toward the goal, trying to meet this goal is not in the best interests of the employee, the company, or the customer. This is an example of how goals can interfere with productivity and seriously detract from meeting the needs of the organization and its stakeholders.

It is also true that goal setting can lead to a very competitive organizational environment. When goals are set in the workplace, this can create competition, and although competition can be a positive and even enjoyable aspect of the work environment, when goal setting creates "dysfunctional" conflict, this can be very harmful to employees and to the organization. For example, if two departments are trying to outproduce one another, and they get so involved with "beating" the other department that they lose sight of the goals and values of the organization, this can lead to things like sabotaging the work of the other department, not sharing information that might be helpful, distorting or lying about productivity or other outcomes, or just pursuing nonessential activities just to "look good" to management. Clearly, none of these things are in the best interest of anyone.

We must also remember that goal setting is also culturally biased; Western cultures often respond well to goal setting, but that is not true of all cultures and that as the workplace becomes more diverse and companies become increasingly global, goal setting can become even more problematic. However, rather than concluding that goal setting is bad, we will conclude that whether goal setting is good or bad depends on the goals, the organization and its culture, the employees and management, how the goals are presented and responded to, the effects that the goals have on individual and organizational performance, and how the goal setting impacts employee job satisfaction. To set and work toward positive and functional goals also means that we need to be aware of the negative and harmful effects that goals can have as well.

Colby Enides, MA, MSW

BIBLIOGRAPHY

Wayne, J. The disadvantages of goals. *Demand Media.* Retrieved April 6, 2016, from http://yourbusiness.azcentral.com/disadvantages-goals -16782.html

Williams, R. (2011). Why goal setting doesn't work. *Psychology Today.* Retrieved April 6, 2016, from www.psychologytoday.com/blog/wired -success/201407/why-goal-setting-doesnt-work

 Controversy #2: Should Employers Take Responsibility for Workers' Stress Management?

INTRODUCTION

Work stress is not something that is new, but there is no question that workers today confront stress daily and over one-third of workers in the United States report high levels of stress, and many more will report moderate to high levels. Because stress has proven to create an increasingly larger burden for employers because of increases in health costs, periods of disability, job turnover, low job satisfaction, and poor productivity, it is very clear that stress is an expensive and destructive problem that affects more than the worker/patient who is the victim of the stress. Some employers look at work stress as a given, and they feel that if employees are not "tough enough" to take it, then they should look for another job. The problem with this archaic way of looking at stress is that it not only creates health problems for the worker but also that the workers who are most likely to leave an organization because of high stress and low morale are the workers who are good enough to get a better job in another company; they will leave first.

It is estimated that American companies pay more than $300 billion per year in health costs, absenteeism, and poor performance that is a direct result of workplace stress. Further, more than 40 percent of job turnover (people leaving for another job) is due to stress, and health costs for employees are 50 percent greater for workers who report high levels of stress. In fact, work stress is the source of more health complaints than financial or family problems combined.

Turnover is expensive for companies, and it is estimated that to replace a single employee will cost the company 120–200 percent of the person's annual salary. Another study found that the cost of absenteeism for a large company is more than $3.6 million per year. One of the common complaints of workers who are dealing with high levels of job stress is depression, and in many companies, this accounts for about 10 sick days per year for employees suffering from depression. Stress even negatively impacts industrial and work-related accidents; insurance company data find that insurance claims for stress-related industrial accidents cost nearly twice as much as nonstress-related industrial accidents.

One thing that the research rarely reports is the impact that work stress has on other aspects of a person's life. Most of the data looks at the health and mental health costs associated with work stress, but there are many other "costs" as well. When people are under stress, it is very difficult to maintain a normal approach to other aspects of their lives. They may be so exhausted from dealing with the stress at work that they may be too tired to play with their children, enjoy relaxing and talking to their spouse or partner, exercising, or just enjoying some pleasant activities. Rarely do people who work in high-stress jobs report a relaxing and healthy life outside of work. Some even dread going on vacation because they know they will not be able to relax and enjoy it, and while they are gone, they will be worrying all the time about what is happening or not happening at work that they will need to deal with when they get back.

Work stress affects both the employee and the organization; so who is responsible for dealing with this problem? Since stress is so expensive for organizations, one would think that this is where the stress management should begin, and although that makes sense, it is not quite as simple as that. For example, the workplace cannot take responsibility for stress that occurs outside of work, and this might be a problem area for some employees; if this is the case, then the employee would have the primary responsibility for managing that type of stress. However, two of the characteristics of stress are that it is cumulative and pervasive. That means that regardless of how hard we may try to leave home problems at home and work problems at work, when we are under significant stress, we carry it around with us. Thus, even if a person is having problems outside of work, the stress from those problems will carry over into the work environment and will affect the worker's performance. Many forward-thinking companies have instituted Employee Assistance Programs (EAPs) that are confidential departments where employees can get advice and support as well as referrals to mental health professionals, medical professionals, lawyers, accountants, and others who can help the person deal with the difficulties in various areas of their lives.

There are other things that employers and companies have found that they can do to reduce work stress, and even if the employee is dealing with stress outside of work, by reducing the work stress, this will help by not complicating the situation and making the cumulative effect of all the stress even worse. Sometimes, companies are reluctant to get involved with the stress management issues of employees because of expense, concerns for privacy, desire to minimize distractions at work, and the complications of managing programs and activities that may appear to be outside of the areas where production and performance are directly involved. However, there are more companies today that are getting involved with these types of issues, but as financial issues emerge, and companies try to be more cost-effective, there is the temptation to cut back on "non-essential" programs and activities.

Globalization, Internet sales, as well as business mergers and acquisitions have made the workplace very different today than it was even a few years ago. Today, all organizations are trying to find ways to be more successful and often even trying to find ways to survive in the business world of the 21st century. On one hand, organizations need to be financially responsible and find ways to keep costs down and improve their sales and services. However, in addition to bringing in customers, organizations need to find ways to attract and retain the best employees, and there is substantial research support as well as experience that demonstrate convincingly that providing a healthy and supportive work environment is the best way to find, hire, and keep the very best employees. Of course, to get and keep the best talent, you also have to pay them fairly and provide reasonable benefits, and unfortunately, many companies try to save money by keeping salaries down and avoiding paying for benefits if they can. However, this approach rarely attracts the best people and will end up costing the company even more in the long run. This is one of the reasons why more companies are looking critically at work conditions and stress issues at work; however, this is not a simple issue.

RESPONSE 1: EMPLOYERS SHOULD TAKE RESPONSIBILITY FOR WORKERS' STRESS MANAGEMENT

Some would question the necessity of employers taking responsibility for the stress management of their employees. However, for many reasons, it is becoming abundantly clear that employers have a substantial investment in their employees managing their own stress responsibly and effectively. Many people (probably most) spend more time at work than they do with their family and friends. Further, for many people, work is one of the main sources of stress in their lives, and therefore learning how to deal with stress effectively at work is a very reasonable goal and one that most companies should take seriously—although most do not seem to do so. Certainly, helping employees deal effectively with stress is good for the employee, but some of the more progressive companies also realize that when employees manage their stress more effectively, it is also very good for business in many ways.

Historically, many companies had a very paternalistic relationship with their employees, and it was assumed that the company would take care of their workers. However, in the past, we were not aware of how dangerous and expensive stress was for workers, and people did not appear to think much about stress, the effects it had, or whose responsibility it was to manage the workplace stress. In more modern times, most companies do not have the type of paternalistic relationship with their employees that they did have in the past, *and* we know much more about stress than we did years ago. However, it is very common today for companies to avoid their responsibilities for employee welfare and health, other than providing a work environment that complies with legal safety requirements, and many companies even complain about that. Today it seems very clear that organizations do have a vested interest in the health, safety, and well-being of their employees and should be more assertive in providing a more stress-free work environment and to help employees learn how to manage their own stress more effectively.

Some companies have begun using programs that will help employees manage workplace and personal/family stress and to help deal with some of difficulties many employees have with managing work-life balance. Things like in-house day care for the children of employees, which may be free or have a very reasonable fee, simplify transportation, save money, and even allow for the parent to see the child during the day on breaks and perhaps even have lunch with the child. Other things include barber and beauty shops, pickup and delivery service for laundry and dry cleaning, financial planning services, health and industrial medicine clinics, walking/biking trails, exercise facilities, and locker rooms to change clothes and clean up. These are examples taken from real companies that are highly successful, pay their employees well, have excellent benefits, and boast very low turnover.

Frequently, employers do not think about how much of the stress at work is unnecessary. For example, jobs should be designed in such a way as to minimize stress; having reasonable hours, decent salary and benefits, some flexibility in work hours when possible, reasonable breaks, a safe and comfortable work environment, good supervision, appropriate training, good communication, frequent and helpful feedback, and many other things are opportunities to reduce stress and foster healthier and more productive employees.

Many companies have also started encouraging healthier lifestyle activities. For example, insisting that people take their breaks and vacations makes a big difference and increases productivity even though people are not working. Activities like weight loss groups, stop-smoking groups, lunchtime walking groups, and many other things cost virtually nothing but are strong signals from the company that they are supporting the employees and are concerned about their health and well-being. The best thing for managers to do is to be good role models for employees, and this refers to healthy behaviors like breaks, vacations, exercise, and having a well-balanced life.

The real answer to the question as to who is responsible for employees' stress management is, "all of the above." Employees must be assertive about their health needs and what they need to do to effectively manage their stress. However, the employers have a real interest in keeping their employees healthy, happy, and productive. The company cannot manage a person's stress for them, but they can provide a safe and healthy workplace, treat employees well and fairly, and provide opportunities for employees to manage their individual stress effectively—this is just good business.

Colby Enides, MA, MSW

BIBLIOGRAPHY

Ivancevich, J. M., Matteson, M. T., Richards, E. P., III. (1985). Who's liable for stress on the job? *Harvard Business Review, 64,* 60–66, 70–72.
Short, K. The employer's responsibility to relieve stress in the workplace. *Chron.* Retrieved May 15, 2017, from http://smallbusiness.chron.com/employers-responsibility-relieve-stress-workplace-13674.html

RESPONSE 2: STRESS MANAGEMENT FOR EMPLOYEES, BY EMPLOYEES

Employees should take the primary responsibility for stress management, rather than simply leaving it up to their employers. Only the employee knows how much stress he or she is under, and we know that individuals each respond to stress differently. Small amounts of stress can be beneficial, but determining the appropriate amount of stress for everyone can be difficult. Employees who have insurance and health benefits through their employer can see doctors to assist with stress in many ways. Because stress is subjective, each person needs to determine what will be best for him or her.

When employees find the best method(s) to relieve their stress, they will increase their autonomy and resilience. Increasing one's autonomy will help people feel more in control of their lives, which will help them manage stress in and outside of work. When people manage their own stress more effectively, they are also more resilient, which means that they will not have as many negative effects from stress and will "bounce back" more quickly from stressful events.

Employer-based stress management programs can be expensive, particularly for small businesses, and employees may not even utilize such programs. Because employees express and handle stress differently, a general program chosen by the employer may not benefit all employees and may not be convenient for some to attend. Regardless of what the employer does regarding workplace stress, if the employee does not take responsibility for his or her own stress management, it will not work anyway. By employees taking responsibility for their own stress management, they will be able to choose an activity that is convenient and best for them.

It is important for employees to take responsibility and find their own work-life balance, which is an important skill to have regardless of the life events or the job they have at the time. There will always be stress, and it is important to have the skills to be able to manage it. In addition, this can be empowering for an individual to determine how best to meet his or her own needs and manage his or her own stress. Taking responsibility for one's own health will benefit the individual both in his or her personal and professional life. Further, if the only thing that an employee does for stress management is on the job, then the stress in the rest of his or her life can still impair performance at work, regardless of the amount of his or her workplace stress.

There are steps that employees can take for managing stress both in and outside of the workplace, and the more of these things that a person does, the better he or she will get at dealing with his or her stress. First, employees can keep a journal documenting stressors and how they respond to them. If there is a pattern of negative responses, such as raising their voice, the employees can look for different, positive ways to respond, such as taking a small break or going for a walk. Second, employees should learn to develop healthy responses to stressors rather than using unhealthy means like overeating or relying on alcohol or other substances to help them cope. Exercise, yoga, hobbies, family/friends time, getting enough sleep, and reducing stimulating activities such as computer and television use at night are key. Third, employees need to establish guidelines for reducing stress by not immediately checking e-mails or texts at home in the evening or not answering the phone or other media during dinner. Fourth, employees need to take time to recharge and engage in nonwork-related activities and make sure they take all their vacation days. Fifth, employees need to learn how to relax using techniques such as meditation, deep breathing exercises, and mindfulness training. These techniques can be used throughout the day and can help employees remain focused both in and outside of the workplace. Sixth, employees should speak to their supervisors if they are feeling stressed at work. This should not be a conversation where the employee lists his or her complaints, but rather an open discussion where the employee and supervisor can develop an effective plan for managing the identified stressor so the employee can maximize his or her performance. Finally, employees should seek support from trusted friends and family who can help them manage their stress, utilize an employee assistance program if one is available, and/or seek a mental health professional. Only the employee knows the amount of stress he or she is under, the best way to manage his or her stress, and he or she needs to take the initiative to deal with his or her stress both in and outside of the workplace.

Liesl A. Nydegger, PhD, MPH

BIBLIOGRAPHY

American Psychological Association. (2017). Coping with stress at work. Retrieved June 5, 2017, from http://www.apa.org/helpcenter/work-stress.aspx

 Controversy #3: Are American Executives Paid Too Much?

INTRODUCTION

There has been considerable discussion in the United States and around the world about the amount of money that corporate CEOs make, and the justifications usually mention things like "salaries are market driven," and, "if you want good people, then you have to pay for them." Certainly, there are examples of CEOs who have turned companies around (not by themselves, of course), and in most cases, they certainly do work long and sometimes challenging hours. However, some question whether or not they are actually worth the money that they get, and some wonder why it is that the CEOs get the credit for the success of companies when it is not even their efforts that produce the results that define the company's achievements.

In addition to the very large salaries, other benefits like bonuses and deferred compensation usually provide considerably more money than their salaries. For example, when Jack Welch was CEO of General Electric, he had an annual salary well up in the seven-figure range. One particular year he was negotiating contracts with the unions in his company, and he showed them the books and said that if GE gave raises in this contract, they would have to lay people off because they couldn't afford it. The unions agreed to not take any raises for the next three years in exchange for the agreement of no layoffs during that time. Although no raises were given to employees, in addition to his salary, Welch was given a $3,000,000 bonus that year. Needless to say, most of the hourly workers felt betrayed and taken advantage of and felt that Welch had been less than honest with them if GE could not afford raises for employees but could afford to give him a very generous bonus.

There was also quite a bit of discussion about Welch's retirement package. Obviously, his salary and benefits had made him a multi-millionaire many times over, but in addition to that, he was given a $417 million retirement package. Further, they gave him the use of an $80,000 per month apartment in Manhattan for as long as he wanted it, courtside seats for the New York Knicks and U.S. Open, seats for Wimbledon, box seats for all home Yankee and Red Sox games, country club fees, security services, and all restaurant charges. Not a bad package for a multimillionaire who could have easily afforded those things on his own. Not many people feel that this is a reasonable benefit and particularly when the raises of the hourly working people have been so small in recent years.

It is interesting that when business people say that executive salaries are market-driven when the executive salaries are determined by the board of directors, most of whom are business people, and clearly the more they pay the CEO, the more they can demand for themselves since they are the ones who are setting the market value of the salaries; this is true in many businesses, including health care. For example, in hospitals and insurance companies, executive salaries usually far outstrip those of the health care providers that actually provide the care and services that hospitals and health insurance companies depend upon. Most physicians have a four-year undergraduate degree, four years of medical school, and then usually a residency, which is usually three or more years depending on the specialty or subspecialty. Most of the executives in health care will have a four-year undergraduate degree, some will have an additional two-year master's degree, and a few will have doctoral-level degrees. Even with less education, in less demanding curricula, the executives in most hospitals and insurance companies will earn more than most of the physicians on their staffs. Many people will not believe this but look at the data—it is true.

It is easy to criticize unfair and ridiculous salaries for executives and particularly for those executives who are not effective. There was one CEO who did a terrible job and his company was heading downhill quickly, largely because of his leadership. His board of directors did not want to scare the investors (and drive stock prices even lower), so they bought out the remainder of his contract and gave him a $5 million bonus for resigning! I would have been upset if I owned stock in that company. However, we also have to look at some of the amazing things that some executives and CEOs have done, and it is hard to argue that they are not worth the money they earn. Historically, people like Thomas Edison, Henry Ford, Clyde Cessna, William Boeing, William Lear, Bill Gates, Mark Zuckerberg, Elon Musk, Lee Iacocca, and many others have made enormous contributions to our world, and it is impossible to even estimate what their contributions have been worth.

The whole notion of executive salaries is very complex and controversial, and there are many opinions about this rather "hot" topic. Very few working people feel that their managers and executives are truly worth the money they are paid, but their opinions have no impact on the decisions that are made about executive compensation. It is also true that the "CEO club" is a small group, and the membership is pretty exclusive. There are many cases of CEOs either leaving or being asked to leave one organization and then very quickly being hired by another and usually for more money than they were making at the first company. The real problem has to do with the ways that corporations are structured and run, and by using boards of directors who have a vested interest in preserving high executive salaries, it is not likely that this will change any time in the near future. An interesting outgrowth of this whole scenario is that in recent years, the executive salaries of not-for-profit organizations have started creeping up as well. Of course, they usually do not match their for-profit contemporaries, but they are much higher than most people realize. The justification for this is the same market-driven logic—if we want good people, we have to pay them what the market demands. It is also true that on many of the nonprofit organizations, many of the people on their boards also come from the business sector and apply the same logic in the nonprofit sector.

RESPONSE 1: SKY HIGH BUT NOT SURE WHY: BLOATED AMERICAN CEO SALARIES

Executive compensation continues to elicit a spirited argument, riddled with divergent opinions about the rationality of pay structure, how deserving these executives are of such lavish rewards, or the overall equity when compared with average or even other highly paid workers. Stories in the media further fuel the fiery debate by reporting on companies underperforming, laying off sizable portions of their workforce, and all while the CEO continues to enjoy rapidly increasing pay raises. Consequently, it is not difficult to understand why this topic has garnered recent attention.

Peter Drucker, one of the most influential management thinkers of our time, once warned that a CEO-to-worker pay ratio greater than 20:1 would create resentment in the employees and send morale plummeting. In the United States, we reached that 20-to-1 ratio back in 1965. To put things in perspective, in 2015, CEOs of large American firms made 276 times more than the average worker. This means that, at an annual salary of approximately $15.5 million, a CEO makes more money in one day than the average worker does in a year, assuming a typical five-day workweek. Stated differently, and perhaps more a compelling assessment, from 1978 to 2015, CEO pay increased 941 percent, whereas the average worker's pay saw a meager increase of only 10 percent. This payment gap between the CEO and typical employee, often called pay dispersion, has seized the attention of academics and the business community alike, further inciting protests and reducing confidence in the fairness of governance practices.

One of the most potentially troubling aspects of CEO compensation, and one that many are surprised to learn, is the way in which top executive pay is set. Because the growth pattern of CEO compensation has surpassed that of profits, the stock market, as well as the top 0.1 percent of wage earners, it is easy for one to assume that it is tied to performance. However, evidence tying executive pay to performance is predominantly inconclusive or weak—at best. In many cases, the relationship between firm performance and CEO pay is completely decoupled. Instead, pay setting processes tend to be murky, covert in nature, and driven by power.

Executives take advantage of their power and position by exerting influence over how the board of directors determines pay structures. Bluntly, it is as if CEOs can set their own pay. The board of directors supervises and sets the pay of the CEO; often a compensation committee of board members will be charged with this responsibility. However, collegial relationships between the executive and board members, as well as the CEO acting as chair of the board, can create an environment of significant influence. Consistently, research has shown that powerful CEOs have higher levels of pay and that boards are reluctant to adjust pay across time (e.g., accounting for years of lesser or better performance). Alternately, there are modern approaches determining CEO compensation where corporations hire consultants to determine executive performance, tie it back to observable metrics, and, subsequently, determine compensation packages. However, the fatal flaw in these models is that the consultants are typically hired by the CEO whom they are evaluating. As such, based on power and their ability to influence the pay setting process, CEOs keep getting raises despite poor performance and declining profits.

While executive pay setting lacks fairness, and arguably fails to work in the best interest of the organization's shareholders, there is little evidence to suggest that CEO compensation will be adequately restrained any time soon. Defenders of the astronomical compensation packages and ambiguous pay setting processes will often cite that it is "market-driven" and that they must compete for those candidates with the best skills. However, this explanation is inconsistent with the data and invites suspicion as most large organizations are susceptible to the power and influence of the CEO, which would drive up the overall industry pay averages. However, recent efforts have been made to moderate such problematic pay practices in the form of new disclosure requirements through the Dodd-Frank Wall Street Reform and Consumer Protection Act of 2010. In addition, peer group comparisons, though inherently flawed given the abovementioned practices, allow shareholder groups to have a "say-on-pay" of the CEO, thus restricting tax breaks for executive performance pay. Hopefully, over time, these efforts will work to readjust executive compensation to a more rational level, reduce employee resentment, increase confidence in systems of governance, and, ultimately, improve company bottom line.

Amber L. Stephenson, PhD, MPH

BIBLIOGRAPHY

Bebchuk, L., & Fried, J. (2004). *Pay without performance: The unfulfilled promise of executive compensation.* Boston, MA: Harvard University Press.

Connelly, B. L., Haynes, K. T., Tiana, L., Gamache, D. L., & Devers, C. E. (2016). Minding the gap: Antecedents and consequences of top management-to-worker pay dispersion. *Journal of Management, 42*(4), 862–885.

Hartung, A. (2015). Why CEOs make so much money. *Forbes.* Retrieved from https://www.forbes.com/sites/adamhartung/2015/06/22/why-ceos-make-so-much-money/#5149675c4203

Huang, R. (2010). Because I'm worth it? CEO pay and corporate governance. *Business Review,* 12–19.

Kerr, J., & Bettis, R. A. (1987). Boards of directors, top management compensation, and shareholder returns. *Academy of Management Journal, 30*(4), 645–664.

Mishel, L., & Schieder, J. (2016). Stock market headwinds meant less generous year for some CEOs. Economic Policy Institute Report. Retrieved from http://www.epi.org/publication/ceo-and-worker-pay-in-2015/

Tosi, H. L., Werner, S., Katz, J. P., & Gomez-Mejia, L. R. (2000). How much does performance matter? A meta-analysis of CEO pay studies. *Journal of Management, 26*(2), 301–339.

Wade, J. B., Porac, J. F., & Pollock, T. G. (1997). Worth, words, and the justification of executive pay. *Journal of Organizational Behavior, 18,* 641–664.

RESPONSE 2: CEO COMPENSATION IS HIGH BUT JUSTIFIABLE

In 2014, it was found that the CEOs in America's largest firms earned $16,316,000 while "typical" workers earned $53,500, a ratio of 303:1. Senator Bernie Sanders voiced concern in an October 2016 tweet, "In 1965, the ratio of CEO pay to average worker pay was 20:1. In 2014, it was 303:1. That's just incomprehensible to me." Other studies report that public opinion surveys conclude that CEOs are vastly overpaid, according to most Americans.

It is also true that CEOs are receiving these big paychecks during a time when both the overall economy and the compensation of typical workers have grown sluggishly. Further, it has never been shown that there is a particularly strong correlation between the compensation of individual CEOs and the performance of their companies. Nonetheless, some would argue that CEOs deserve their high compensation for many reasons.

First, it is important to be clear as to what is meant by "CEO salaries." The $16 million CEOs took home in 2014 was not an actual paycheck. XYZ Corp. did not pay CEO Jones a salary of $16 million. CEOs do receive salaries and fringe benefits, but the median value of their salaries is about $1.5 million. The bulk of the compensation consists of various sorts of incentive pay, including bonuses, restricted stock grants (stock given to the CEO only if certain goals are met), and stock options. The extremely large paydays for CEOs, such as Michael Eisner of Disney's $570 million in 1997, have come about because of their taking advantage of incentive pay clauses, and this is not an annual event.

Although some feel that it is almost "criminal" to make such gigantic salaries, there are some points to consider:

First, private corporations make compensation decisions, and if the CEO makes "too much," it is the shareholders who suffer the consequences in terms of a reduced return. While society does have a stake in the matter since CEO compensation is considered a deductible expense on the corporate tax, society has already spoken over two decades ago, limiting the maximum tax deduction to $1,000,000 a year; however, this has not put an end to the high levels of CEO compensation.

Second, extraordinarily high levels of CEO compensation might be considered an efficient solution to a host of problems. It would be difficult to convince someone to take on the headaches associated with being responsible for the well-being of thousands of employees and stockholders, many communities, and even entire nations, being on call 24/7/365, and being the oft-vilified public face of a large organization; a generous financial package might certainly ease the pain.

CEOs are typically recruited from those already highly placed in the corporate job ladder. Given the difficulties of the CEO positions, it might be challenging to convince already highly paid executives to leave their comfortable position for a new set of even bigger headaches. The Tournament Model would solve this problem with a lopsided pay bump. Some are concerned about CEO salaries as working against the best interest of the stakeholders in the organization, but one way to solve the principal/agent problem of aligning the goals of the CEO with those of the stockholders would be offering the CEO inducements based on the achievement of certain long-term goals, including, but not necessarily limited to, pushing up the stock price.

Third, the CEO compensation and ratio numbers used above can be misleading. The $16 million compensation figure is based on 350 CEOs, but there are approximately 1.7 million C corporations (the traditional stock issuing organizations) in the country, and they all have a chief executive. It appears to be unreasonable to compare the compensation of the top 0.02 percent of all CEOs to the average of all workers.

Unfortunately, no database has complete compensation data from all corporations, but there are more comprehensive sources of information available. For example, the Bureau of Labor Statistics (BLS) annually publishes "Occupational Employment and Wages: Chief Executives," and it was found that in 2014, the average chief executive earned $180,700 and the ratio was about 4:1—far different than the 303:1 reported above.

One can quibble with this data, since many of the private firms in the BLS sample are smaller than typical, and many are in the public sector or are religious organizations, advocacy groups, or labor unions. However, the real point is that the corporate landscape is a diverse one. This makes it very difficult to determine to whom a given CEO should be compared. Clearly, the issue of CEO salaries is far more complex than simple headlines would have us believe.

Robert S. Rycroft, PhD

BIBLIOGRAPHY

Bureau of Labor Statistics. (2015). Occupational employment and wages, May 2015: 11–1011 chief executives. Occupational Employment Statistics. Retrieved April 25, 2017, from https://www.bls.gov/oes/2015/may/oes111011.htm

Fisher, A. (2015). CEO pay: Flatter salaries, but bigger bonuses. *Fortune*, September 2. Retrieved June 16, 2017, from http://fortune.com/2015/09/02/ceo-pay-flatter-salaries-but-bigger-bonuses/

Larcker, D. F., Donatiello, N. E., & Tayan, B. (2016). Americans and CEO pay: 2016 public perception survey on CEO compensation. CGRI Survey Series. Corporate Governance Research Initiative, Stanford Rock Center for Corporate Governance. Retrieved June 15, 2017, from https://www.gsb.stanford.edu/faculty-research/publications/americans-ceo-pay-2016-public-perception-survey-ceo-compensation

Lazear, E. P., & Rosen, S. (1981). Rank-order tournaments as optimum labor contracts. *Journal of Political Economy*, 89(5), 841–864.

Mishel, L., & Davis, A. (2015). Top CEOs make 300 time more than typical workers. Economic Policy Institute Issue Brief #399. Retrieved June 14, 2017, from http://www.epi.org/publication/top-ceos-make-300-times-more-than-workers-pay-growth-surpasses-market-gains-and-the-rest-of-the-0-1-percent/

Perry, M. J. (2015). When we consider all US "Chief Executives," the "CEO-to-Worker Pay Ratio" falls from 331:1 to below 4:1. *AEI Ideas (American Enterprise Institute blog)*, May 1. Retrieved June 14, 2017,

from https://www.aei.org/publication/when-we-consider-all-us-chief
-executives-the-ceo-to-worker-pay-ratio-falls-from-3311-to-below-41/

Perry, M. J. (2017). More on the statistical chicanery of the AFL-CIO's
artificially inflated CEO-to-worker pay ratio. *AEI Ideas (American
Enterprise Institute blog)*, June 1. Retrieved June 14, 2017, from https://
www.aei.org/publication/more-on-the-statistical-chicanery-of-the-afl
-cios-artificially-inflated-ceo-to-worker-pay-ratio/

Directory of Resources

BOOKS AND ARTICLES

Blustein, D. L. (2006). *The psychology of working*. Mahwah, NJ: Lawrence Erlbaum Associates.

Blustein, D. L. (2014). *The oxford handbook of the psychology of working*. Oxford, UK: Oxford University Press.

Blustein, D. L., Kenna, A. C., Gill, N., & DeVoy, J. E. (2008). The psychology of working: A new framework for counseling practice and public policy. *The Career Development Quarterly*, 56, 294–308.

Bridgestock, L. (2014). Differences in average working hours around the world. Retrieved from https://www.topuniversities.com/blog/differences-average-working-hours-around-world

Burnette, J. L., & Pollack, J. M. (2013). Implicit theories of work and job fit: Implications for job and life satisfaction.*Basic and Applied Social Psychology*, 35(4), 360–372.

Camarota, S. A., & Ziegler, K. (2009, August). Jobs Americans won't do? A detailed look at immigrant employment by occupation. Retrieved from http://cis.org/illegalImmigration-employment

Cronin, B. (2013). Who treats their workers best? *The Wall Street Journal*. Retrieved from http://blogs.wsj.com/economics/2013/10/01/who-treats-their-workers-best/

Gill, F. (1999). The meaning of work: Lessons from sociology, psychology, and political theory. *The Journal of Socio-Economics*, 28, 725–743.

Hackman, J. R., & Oldham, G. R. (1980). *Work redisign*. Reading, MA: Addison-Wesley.

Hofstede, G. (1984). *Culture's consequences: International differences in work-related values* (2nd ed.). Beverly Hills, CA: SAGE Publications.

Howell, W. C. (1976). *Essentials of industrial and organizational psychology*. Homewood, IL: Dorsey Press.

Karasek, R. A., & Theorell, T. (1990). *Healthy work: Stress, productivity, and the reconstruction of working life*. New York, NY: Basic Books.

Miller, G. E. (2017). The U.S. is the most overworked developed nation in the world—when do we draw the line? Retrieved from https://20somethingfinance.com/american-hours-worked-productivity-vacation/

Nisen, M. (2013). The 10 countries with the world's best workers. *Business Insider*. Retrieved from http://www.businessinsider.com/countries-with-the-best-workers-2013-10

Rayton, B. A., & Yalabik, Z. Y. (2014). Work engagement, psychological contract breach and job satisfaction. *Journal of Human Resource Management, 25*(17), 2382–2400.

Shah, R. (2014). "The culture map" shows us the differences in how we work worldwide. Retrieved from http:/www.forbes.com/sites/rawnshah/2014/10/06/the-culture-map-shows-us-how-we-work-worldwide/#6e6ed12a6ed12a6e4f

Turner, N., Barling, J., & Zacharatos, A. (2002). Positive psychology at work. *Handbook of Positive Psychology, 52*, 715–728.

Twenge, J. M. (2016). Do millennials have a lesser work ethic? *Psychology Today*. Retrieved from www.psychologytoday.com/blog/our-changing-culture/201602/do-millennials-have-lesser-work-ethic

Twenge, J. M., Campbell, S. M., Hoffman, B. J., & Lance, C. E. (2010). Generational differences in work Values: Leisure and extrinsic values increasing, social and intrinsic values decreasing. *Journal of Management, 36*(5), 1117–1142.

ORGANIZATIONS AND WEBSITES

AGE Platform Europe

http://www.age-platform.eu/

This site shows what many of the Western European countries are doing about issues with the aging population, and shows the kinds of concerns that they have. It also gives examples of programs that we might consider in the U.S. as well.

American Federation of Labor-Congress of Industrial Organizations (AFL-CIO)

https://aflcio.org/

American labor unions have traditionally supported workers' rights, and with the population of workers increasing in age, these groups have started paying more attention to issues involving older workers and retirees.

American Psychological Association

http://www.apa.org/

This organization has articles and references to many different sites that have recent scholarly and professional information about psychological topics involving work and organizations.

Occupational Safety and Health Administration

http://osha.gov

This governmental agency establishes regulations and guidelines identifying what organizations are responsible for providing to ensure safe and healthy work environments.

Society for Industrial and Organizational Psychology

http://www.siop.org/

This society is part of the American Psychological Association and is primarily concerned with psychological factors in people and organizations. They sponsor and support research and scholarship in these areas.

U.S. Department of Labor

http://www.dol.gov

This governmental department represents the laws and regulations that are in place to protect workers and consumers. This site has links to many different sources of information about issues related to work and workers.

U.S. Equal Employment Opportunity Commission

https://www.eeoc.gov/

This commission is responsible for enforcing equal employment rights for all workers and potential employees. They also have many articles and sources to provide information about worker and employee rights.

Glossary

Absenteeism: The habitual nonpresence of an employee at his or her job, or a student from his or her school.

Agriculture: The science, art, or occupation dealing with cultivating land, raising crops, and feeding, breeding, and raising livestock; the practice of agriculture is farming.

Allies: The victorious nations of World War I and World War II that worked together to defeat the *Axis* nations. In World War I, the *Allies* included Britain, France, Italy, Russia, and the United States. In World War II, the *Allies* included Britain, France, the Soviet Union, and the United States.

Anthropologist: A person who specializes in anthropology, which is the science of the origins, physical and cultural development, biological characteristics, and social customs and beliefs of human beings and their groups.

Archeology: The scientific study of material remains (e.g., fossil relics, artifacts, and monuments) of past human life and activities.

Archetypes: In Jungian psychology, a collectively inherited unconscious idea, pattern of thought, image, and so forth, universally present in all people's minds.

Asynchrony: When events do not occur at the same time.

Autonomy: Being independent of thought and action; in human resource management it refers to a degree or level of freedom and discretion for an employee over his or her job.

Baby boomers: People born between 1946 and 1964; following World War II when soldiers came home, the birth rate increased significantly.

Behavior modification: A collection of techniques and methods for changing a person's (or animal's) behavior; widely used in a variety of situations, including the workplace; usually associated with operant/Skinnerian conditioning.

Behavior potential: In Julian Rotter's cognitive theory, the likelihood that a specific behavior will occur in a given situation.

Behavior therapy: A collection of techniques and methods for changing a person's (or other animal's) behavior; typically applied to the modification of abnormal behavior; usually associated with classical/Pavlovian conditioning.

Bottom line: In business, the last line in an audit or financial report that shows profit or loss. It also refers to the final, determining consideration in a decision.

Bullying: The use (or threat of use) of superior strength or influence to intimidate a person or group to force him/her/them to do what the bullying person wants them to do.

Burnout: Occupational burnout is characterized by exhaustion, lack of enthusiasm, decreased motivation, and feelings of ineffectiveness. This may also result in frustration or cynicism and thus reduced effectiveness in the workplace.

Capitalism: An economic theory in which a society's means of production is held by private individuals or organizations, and not the government;

prices, distribution of goods, and products are determined by the free market.

Career: A person's occupation or profession followed as one's lifework; usually involves specific training and/or education.

Caregiver work: Caregiver work refers to jobs like home health aide or visiting nurse whose main job is taking care of other people. A caregiver is a person who gives assistance to people who are sick, injured, mentally or physically disabled, or are elderly and/or fragile.

Child labor: Work that deprives children of their childhood and is harmful to their physical and mental development. Children are forced or allowed to work in industry rather than having a normal childhood; it is illegal in most countries.

Civil defense: People who are not part of the military but are trained to protect and help communities if an enemy attacks their country or if there is a natural disaster.

Classical/Pavlovian conditioning: A type of conditioning or learning where a neutral stimulus is paired with another stimulus that already produces a response, and that after the pairing, the neutral stimulus now also produces a response.

Cognitive: Any mental process involving conscious intellectual activity; for example, thinking, perceiving, learning, deciding, remembering, and so forth.

Cognitive restructuring: A psychological technique usually associated with cognitive behavioral therapy, where a psychologist helps a person learn to think differently about an issue, event, or person.

Cold War: A constant, nonviolent state of hostility between the Soviet Union and the United States, which began shortly after World War II, with the rapid extension of Soviet influence over Eastern Europe and North Korea, ending in the breakup of the Soviet Union in 1991.

Collective unconscious: From the psychological theory of Carl Jung; refers to thoughts, feelings, images, and the like that are shared by all people and relate to elements from the common heritage of the entire human race.

Collectivism: The political principle of centralized social and economic control by the government; the welfare of the many is seen to be more important than the rights or privileges of the individual.

Communism: A system or theory of social organization in which all property, industry, governmental agencies, police, military, and economic institutions are owned and controlled by society or a single-party government.

Computer-mediated communication: Communication systems that occur through computer systems. People do not communicate directly but only by using computer systems to facilitate and enable the communication.

Conditioned response: A response made by a person or animal after learning to associate a behavior with a neutral or arbitrary stimulus.

Conditioned stimulus: In classical/Pavlovian conditioning, the conditioned stimulus is a previously neutral stimulus that, after becoming associated with a stimulus that produces a response, will trigger a new, conditioned response.

Conditions of worth: In Rogerian psychological theory, people learn that they must behave in certain ways if they are to feel that others value them; this is typically behavior that the person would not choose to do themselves.

Consciousness: Awareness or perception of an inner psychological or spiritual fact: knowledge of something in one's inner self.

Control freak: A person who feels and acts like he or she needs to control everything and everyone around them.

Cross-sectional research: Research where you study the differences between age groups by studying groups of people of different ages at the same point in time.

Culture: The cumulative knowledge, experience, beliefs, values, attitudes, norms, notions of time, roles, concepts of the universe, and material objects and possessions acquired by a group of people or society, and it is passed from one generation to the next.

Denial: From Freudian psychoanalysis; a psychological defense where a person denies that he or she thought, felt, or behaved in a way that was counter to the norms of society and/or the person's own values or conscience.

Depression: A psychiatric condition that involves a sad mood, feelings of helplessness and hopelessness, sleeping problems, changes in appetite, social withdrawal, fatigue, lack of motivation, and lack of pleasure in things that were formerly enjoyable.

Discrimination: The unjust treatment of different categories of people frequently on the grounds of race, age, religious background, or sex.

Dust Bowl: Land where vegetation has been lost and soil reduced to dust and eroded, especially because of drought or unsuitable farming practices. Found in Kansas, Oklahoma, and northern Texas in the 1930s.

Economist: An expert who studies the relationship between a society's resources and its production or output. The societies may range from the smallest local community to an entire nation or even the global economy.

Ego: From Freudian psychoanalysis, the "adaptive organ" of personality that helps the person meet his or her needs within the constraints of his or her conscience and of society.

Employee: A person who works part- or full-time under an employment contract, whether oral or written, expressed or implied, who has established rights and duties.

Empowerment: To give power to another person. To give official authority or legal power to an employee to make decisions about his or her job and how he or she fulfills his or her responsibilities.

Executive: Person or group appointed and given the responsibility to manage the affairs of an organization and the authority to make decisions within specified boundaries. May also refer to the branch of an organization or government.

Existentialism: A philosophical theory that emphasizes the existence of the individual person as a free and responsible agent determining his or her own life through acts of will.

Expectancy: From Julian Rotter's cognitive theory, the subjective probability that a specific behavior will result in a given outcome.

Extinction: From operant and classical conditioning theories, when a reward or reinforcement is ceased, the behavior that was supported by the reward/reinforcement will die out.

Feedback: When dealing with the performance of an employee, this refers to helpful information or criticism that is given to someone to suggest what can be done to improve performance, a product, and so forth.

Femininity: A set of attributes, behaviors, and roles generally associated with girls and women. Femininity is a factor in every culture, including both socially defined and biologically created factors.

Flextime: A nontraditional work scheduling practice, which allows full-time employees to choose their individual starting and quitting times within certain limits. Flextime periods are usually before or after a core time during which all employees must be present; it is expected that the employee will work the same number of hours as he or she would on a normal work schedule.

Generation X: People born between 1965 and 1979.

GI Bill: A law passed in 1944 that provided educational and other benefits for people who had served in the armed forces in World War II. The benefits are available to all service people who were honorably discharged.

Glass ceiling: An intangible barrier within an organizational hierarchy that prevents women or minorities from getting upper-level positions.

Global job satisfaction: A general attitude that an employee has about his or her overall satisfaction with his or her job.

Globalization: The interaction and integration of the people, companies, and governments of different nations driven by international trade and investment and aided by information technology.

Great Depression: The economic crisis and below-normal business activity in the United States and other countries, beginning with the stock market crash in October 1929 and continuing throughout most of the 1930s.

Hierarchical: An arrangement (e.g., people in a group, also things) in order of rank, importance, and so forth.

Humanism: A philosophical approach that attaches prime importance to human being rather than divine or supernatural agencies. Humanists believe in the potential value and goodness of human beings, emphasize common human needs, and seek solely rational ways of solving human problems.

Id: In Freudian psychoanalysis, the fundamental "organ" of personality with which all people are born. It is the repository of all sexual and aggressive instincts and is the basis for all psychic energy.

Identity: The set of characteristics by which an individual is recognizable as an individual member of a group. The distinct and persisting personality of an individual; a person's individuality.

Individualism: A philosophical approach that maintains the political and economic independence of the individual and stresses individual initiative, action, and interests.

Indulgent: Willing to allow excessive leniency, generosity, or consideration.

Industrial/Organizational Psychology: A branch of psychology involved with research and teaching about people and groups in organizations; also, deals with the functioning of organizations and how to help them be more effective, efficient, safer, and supportive of employees.

Industrialization: When industry and manufacturing are introduced on a large scale to a region or country.

Information revolution: The explosion of availability of information resulting from the use of computers, other electronic devices, and the Internet.

Innate valuing tendency: From Rogerian personality theory, the inherent factor that enables all people to evaluate the quality of their life experiences relative to their own true self-interest and identity.

Job: A paid position of regular employment.

Job description: A broad, general, and written statement of a specific job that includes duties, purpose, responsibilities, and scope; specifies working conditions, the job's title, and the person to whom the employee reports.

Job facet satisfaction: An employee's attitude about a specific aspect (facet) of his or her job.

Job satisfaction: An attitude that one has about his or her job that indicates how positively or negatively he or she feels about his or her job.

Job security: The assurance that a person will keep his or her job without the risk of becoming unemployed.

Karōshi: A Japanese term referring to death resulting from overwork.

Labor union: An organization typically comprised by workers from the same trade or similar trades formed for advancing its members' interests through collective bargaining with respect to wages, benefits, and working conditions.

Layoff: The temporary or permanent removal of a worker from his or her job, typically, due to cutbacks in production or corporate reorganization.

Leadership: The position or function of a person who guides or directs a group and who has influence over the group members and their activities.

Locus of control: The extent to which people feel they have control over the events that influence their lives. A person with "internal" locus of control believes he or she is primarily responsible for things that happen to him or her; a person with "external" locus of control believes that things which happen to him or her are due primarily to external factors (e.g., luck, chance, fate, other people).

Longitudinal research: Research looking at age differences by studying the same group of people over time and at different ages.

Long-term orientation: A trait of a person or a characteristic of an organizational or national culture whereby decisions and operations are primarily directed to optimizing future outcomes.

Manager: A person responsible for and who has the authority for controlling or administering all or part of a company or other type of organization.

Masculinity: Possession of the qualities usually associated with men.

Micromanaging: When managers get unnecessarily involved in some of the minor elements of an employee's job.

Millennials: People born between 1980 and 1994.

Modeling: A form of learning where individuals learn how to act or perform by observing another individual. Modeling is a cognitive type of social learning.

Morale: The mental and emotional condition (e.g., enthusiasm, confidence, or loyalty) of an individual or group regarding the function or tasks they are involved with and/or the organization or group of which they are a part.

Motivation: Internal and external factors that stimulate a desire and willingness to expend energy in people to continue to be interested and committed to a job, role, or subject, and to make an effort to attain a goal or objective.

Neo-Freudian: A psychodynamic theorist following Freud who had a theory that deviated from the original psychoanalytic approach.

Neurosis: Sometimes called psychoneurosis, a functional (nonorganic) disorder involving feelings of anxiety, obsessional thoughts, compulsive acts, and physical complaints without objective evidence of disease that could dominate the personality.

Nonviolent aggression: Behavior intended to harm another person, animal, or other entity (e.g., an organization or government) but is not physically violent; slander, harassment, bullying, and the like.

Norms: Informal guidelines about what is considered "normal" (what is correct or incorrect) social behavior in a particular group, organization, or other social unit.

Operant/Skinnerian conditioning: A type of learning based on the work of Skinner, where behavior is a function of its consequences. Reinforcement is the fundamental concept, and this is anything that increases the probability of a behavior recurring (e.g., a reward).

Organizational behavior modification: Behavior modification typically using operant/Skinnerian conditioning in an organizational setting; designed to modify the behavior of people and groups in the organization.

Organized crime: A group that has a corporate structure and whose primary objective is to obtain money through illegal activities; usually relying on fear and corruption as means of influence.

Person-job fit: This refers to how well a person "fits" into his or her job; is a predictor of how well a person performs in his or her job.

Person-organization fit: This refers to how well a person "fits" into the organization he or she is working in; that is, how well the person becomes part of the organizational culture. This is a better predictor of job success in the long-run than person-job fit.

Pessimistic: The tendency to see, anticipate, or emphasize only bad or undesirable outcomes, results, conditions, and problems. This type of person will typically expect the worst outcome in any given situation.

Phobia: A persistent, abnormal, and irrational fear of a specific thing or situation that leads one to avoid the feared stimulus. Phobias are generally learned by conditioning and/or observational learning.

Posttraumatic stress disorder (PTSD): A psychological condition that is caused by a terrifying event that is either experienced or witnessed. Symptoms usually include flashbacks, nightmares, severe anxiety, and uncontrollable thoughts about the event.

Power distance: A concept from Hofstede's theory about cultural differences that describes how people belonging to a specific culture view power relationships between people, including the degree to which people not in power accept that power is spread unequally.

Power monger: A person who tries to accumulate power for power's sake. Power mongers attempt to gain power in all or most situations and typically see most relationships in power terms.

Preconscious: From Freudian psychoanalysis; refers to things that are not in one's consciousness but can be brought to consciousness simply by focusing on it. For example, "What did you have for dinner last night?" You may not have been thinking about it, but by directing your attention you can bring it into consciousness.

Prejudice: A negative opinion or feeling that a person has beforehand or without knowledge, thought, or reason; any preconceived attitude or feeling, either favorable or unfavorable. Prejudice usually involves unreasonable feelings, opinions, or attitudes, especially of a hostile nature, regarding an ethnic, racial, social, or religious group.

Presenteeism: When an employee comes to work when he or she is ill, injured, or significantly emotionally upset; the employee is unable to perform his or her job at an appropriate level and may actually harm the organization and/or other employees.

Profession: A paid occupation; especially one that involves prolonged education and training and usually has a formal qualification.

Profitability: The ability of a business to earn a profit. A profit is what remains after a business pays all expenses directly related to the generation of the revenue.

Psyche: A person's center of thought, feeling, and motivation; the psyche consciously and unconsciously directs the body's responses to its social and physical environment.

Psychiatrist: A physician (either an MD or DO) who after completing medical school will have additional training (a residency) to gain more expertise in the diagnosis and treatment of mental health problems. Psychiatric treatment usually involves the prescription of medications and can also utilize other medical treatments like electroconvulsive shock therapy.

Psychoanalysis: Originally begun by Sigmund Freud, a system of psychological theory and therapy that aims to treat mental disorders by investigating the interaction of conscious and unconscious elements in the mind. It attempts to bring repressed fears and conflicts into the conscious mind where they can be resolved using techniques like dream interpretation and free association.

Psychodynamic: The study of the interaction of conscious and unconscious mental or emotional processes; especially as they influence personality, thoughts, feelings, behavior, and attitudes.

Psychological contract: A set of "promises" or "expectations" between the parties in an employment relationship. Unlike formal contracts of employment, these are usually tacit or implicit.

Psychological defense: A variety of unconscious mental processes used to protect oneself from shame, anxiety, loss of self-esteem, conflict, or other unacceptable feelings or thoughts.

Psychologist: A doctoral mental health professional; usually with a PhD, PsyD, or EdD who is involved with the field of psychology. They may do research, teach, or diagnose and treat mental disorders depending on their specialty. Clinical and counseling psychologists frequently work with patients and treat psychological conditions. Although some psychologists are trained and licensed to also prescribe medication, most psychologists use nonmedical forms of treatment like psychotherapy.

Psychopathology: Abnormal psychological states or conditions; also, the field that studies abnormal psychological disorders.

Psychosocial development: A theory usually associated with Erik Erikson that looks at psychological development from the standpoint of social development; unlike Freudian theory that looks at psychosexual development.

Racketeering: Obtaining or extorting money illegally or carrying on illegal business activities; frequently associated with organized crime. Illegal activity carried out as an enterprise owned or controlled by those who are engaged in the illegal activity.

Rat race: An exhausting, unremitting, and usually competitive activity or routine; often associated with a pressured urban working life spent trying to get ahead with little time left for anything other than work.

Reinforcement: Anything following a response that increases the likelihood of the response being repeated; for example, a reward.

Repression: A psychological defense in which unpleasant or frightening impulses, images, thoughts, feelings, or memories are put into the unconscious and are not experienced directly by the conscious mind.

Self: The "core" of personality; a person's essential being that distinguishes them from all others. The object of introspection or "self-awareness."

Self-actualization: Primarily from the theory of Abraham Maslow and other humanist theorists, it is the inherent need for all people to become the best person of which they are capable.

Self-identity: How a person "sees" or conceives of himself or herself.

Sexual harassment: Unwelcome sexual advances, including requests for sexual favors, and other verbal or physical conduct of a sexual nature that creates an offensive or hostile work environment. This is a form of sex discrimination that occurs in the workplace.

Short-term orientation: A personal trait or characteristic of an organization, group, or culture that focuses on optimizing the short-range goals and outcomes with less consideration given for longer-term issues or goals.

Social connectedness: The measure of how people get together and interact. Social connectedness involves the quality and number of connections one has with other people in a relevant social circle.

Social contract: A usually implicit agreement between individuals and the group, community, or governing entity of which they are a part. The agreement usually involves people giving up some of their individual rights in exchange for the benefits and protection available to members of the group.

Social Learning Theory: Originally associated with Albert Bandura, it involves a type of cognitive and behavioral learning that relies on things like observational and other nonbehavioral forms of learning in social conditions.

Socialism: A political and economic theory that advocates that the means of production, distribution, and exchange goods and services should be owned or regulated by the community.

Social-reference group: A social group to whom one refers oneself or compares oneself to; a group that is important to the individual.

Sociologist: An expert in the development, structure, and functioning of human society.

Status: The relative position or rank of someone or something in relation to others in a relevant society, organization, or group.

Stress: A psychological and physical response that the body makes to changes or demands confronting the person; stress can occur because of negative or positive factors.

Subconscious: Frequently used interchangeably with "unconscious" and used as an important concept in Freudian psychoanalysis and other psychodynamic theories. It refers to instincts, thoughts, feelings, memories, trauma, and other factors that are not available directly to the conscious mind.

Sublimation: From Freudian psychoanalysis, a psychological defense whereby anxiety produced by subconscious desires, needs, ideas, and so forth is reduced when the subconscious factors are converted to socially acceptable alternative thoughts, feelings, or behaviors.

Subordinate: Someone or something that is in an inferior position relative to another relevant person or thing. For example, an employee is a subordinate to his or her boss.

Superego: From Freudian psychoanalysis, one of the organs of personality where the person has learned the norms, values, and expectations of society, and this becomes the conscience and "ideal" of the person.

The superego forms when the child learns societies' "rules" through their interaction with their parents or parenting figures.

Superego ideal: From Freudian psychoanalysis, the ideal in the subconscious part of the the superego that represents the inner self that a person would strive to become.

Supervisor: A person who oversees, instructs, and evaluates the work, behavior, or performance of another person or employee.

Team-based management: A system of work whereby the goals and tasks of an organization are made to a team rather than to individual employee and the team decides how to fulfill the expectations. Rewards and feedback are likewise provided to the team. Individual supervision and feedback may be provided but are secondary to those provided to the team.

Telecommuting: An arrangement between some employees and some organizations where the employee can do his or her work at home; frequently involves the use of computers and phones.

Tennessee Valley Authority (TVA): A federal agency created in 1933 by President Franklin Roosevelt to create jobs and provide cheaper electricity during the Great Depression. It controls the electricity, irrigation, and flood control from the dams and reservoirs along the Tennessee River.

Traditionalists: People born between 1900 and 1945.

Uncertainty avoidance: A personal trait or quality of a culture where people seek certainty and avoid risk.

Unconditioned response: A response that does not have to be learned; it occurs reliably in response to a specific stimulus.

Unconditioned stimulus: A stimulus that reliably produces a given response; an automatic response and the stimulus-response connection does not have to be learned.

Unconscious: Below or absent from the consciousness; see "subconscious."

Virtual work team: A work team that is not colocated (not all members are in the same place). They work and communicate largely through computer-mediated communication; they will usually work "asynchronously" (not at the same time).

Voluntary turnover: When people leave a job for their own reasons rather than being fired or laid off.

WACS: The Women's Army Corp was formed in World War II to provide support for noncombat military positions (e.g., secretarial and clerical).

WAVES: Women Accepted for Volunteer Emergency Service was the World War II women's branch of the U.S. Naval Reserve.

Work: An activity involving mental or physical effort done with intent of fulfilling a purpose or accomplishing a result.

Work engagement: A positive and fulfilling work-related mental state characterized by vigor, dedication, and absorption.

Workaholic: A person who has a compulsive and unrelenting need to work to the exclusion of other activities that would lead to a full and well-balanced life. Workaholics seem to feel that if they are not working then they are only wasting time.

Workers' compensation: A form of insurance providing wage and medical benefits to employees injured on the job. By using this insurance, the worker must accept the mandatory relinquishment of his or her right to sue his or her employer for negligence.

Working poor: People who are working but whose income places them below the poverty line; they are often without medical insurance or other benefits usually provided for employees.

Works Progress Administration (WPA): Begun by Franklin Delano Roosevelt in the 1930s, it was the largest American New Deal agency employing millions of people (mostly unskilled men) to carry out public works projects (renamed in 1939 as the Work Projects Administration).

Bibliography

CHAPTER 1

Blustein, D. L. (2006). *The psychology of working*. Mahwah, NJ: Lawrence Erlbaum Associates.

Blustein, D. L., Kenna, A. C., Gill, N., & DeVoy, J. E. (2008). The psychology of work: A new framework for counseling practice and public policy. *The Career Development Quarterly, 56*, 294–308.

Gill, F. (2016). The meaning of work: Lessons from sociology, psychology, and political theory. Retrieved from http://citeseerx.ist.psu.edu/viewdoc/summary?doi=10.1.1.335.6207

Goldstein, J. (2012). What America does for work. Retrieved from http://www.npr.org/sections/money/2012/03/20/149015363/what-america-does-for-work

Rayton, B. A., & Yalabik, Z. Y. (2014). Work engagement, psychological contract breach and job satisfaction. *Journal of Human Resource Management, 25*(17), 2382–2400.

CHAPTER 2

Blustein, D. L. (2006). *The psychology of working*. Mahwah, NJ: Lawrence Erlbaum Associates.

Blustein, D. L., Kenna, A. C., Gill, N., & DeVoy, J. E. (2008). The psychology of work: A new framework for counseling practice and public policy. *The Career Development Quarterly, 56,* 294–308.

Gill, F. (2016). The meaning of work: Lessons from sociology, psychology, and political theory. Retrieved from http://citeseerx.ist.psu.edu/viewdoc/summary?doi=10.1.1.335.6207

Goldstein, J. (2012). What America does for work. Retrieved from http://www.npr.org/sections/money/2012/03/20/149015363/what-america-does-for-work

Wier, K. (2013). More than job satisfaction. American Psychological Association. Retrieved from http://www.apa.org/monitor/2013/12/job-satisfaction.aspx

CHAPTER 3

Bettelley, C. (2013). How employers should manage workplace stress. Retrieved from http://www.employeebenefits.co.uk/how-employers-should-manage-workplace-stress/

Blustein, D. L. (2006). *The psychology of working.* Mahwah, NJ: Lawrence Erlbaum Associates.

Blustein, D. L., Kenna, A. C., Gill, N., & DeVoy, J. E. (2008). The psychology of working: A new framework for counseling practice and public policy. *The Career Development Quarterly, 56,* 294–308.

Burnette, J. L., & Pollack, J. M. (2013). Implicit theories of work and job fit: Implications for job and life satisfaction. *Basic and Applied Social Psychology, 35*(4), 360–372.

Cronin, B. (2013). Who treats their workers best? *Wall Street Journal.* Retrieved from http://blogs.swj.com/economics/2013/10/01/who-treats-their-workers-best/

Health and Safety Executive. (2016). Who is responsible for tackling work related stress in the organization? Retrieved from http://www.hse.gov.uk/stress/furtheradvice/responsible.htm

Ivancevich, J. M., Matteson, M. T., & Richards, E. P., III. (1985). Who's liable for stress on the job? *Harvard Business Review.* Retrieved from https://hbr.org/1985/03/whos-liable-for-stress-on-the-job

Karasek, R. A., & Theorell, T. (1990). *Healthy work: Stress, productivity, and the reconstruction of working life.* New York, NY: Basic Books.

Lee, S., McCann, D., & Messenger, J. C. (2007). *Working time around the world: Trends in working hours, laws and policies in a global comparative perspective.* London: ILO/Routledge.

Miller, G. E. (2017). The U.S. is the most overworked developed nation in the world—when do we draw the line? Retrieved from https://20some thingfinance.com/american-hours-worked-productivity-vacation/

Rayton, B. A., & Yalabik, Z. Y. (2014). Work engagement, psychological contract breach and job satisfaction. *The International Journal of Human Resource Management, 25*(17), 2382–2400.

Segal, J., Smith, M., Robinson, L., & Segal, R. (2017). Stress in the workplace. *Helpguide.org.* Retrieved from https://www.helpguide.org/articles/ stress/stress-at-work.htm

Semmer, N. K., Jacobshagen, N., Meier, L. L., Elferint, A., Beehr, T. A., Kälin, W., & Tschan, F. (2015). Illegitimate tasks as a source of work stress. *Work & Stress: An International Journal of Work, Health & Organisations, 29*(1), 32–56.

Turner, N., Barling, J., & Zacharatos, A. (2002). Positive psychology at work. *Handbook of Positive Psychology, 52,* 715–728.

UMass Lowell. Financial costs of job stress. Retrieved from https://www .uml.edu/Research/CPH-NEW/Worker/stress-at-work/financial-costs .aspx

Weir, K. (2013). More than job satisfaction. *APA Monitor, 44*(1), 39.

CHAPTER 4

Adler Graduate School. (2017). Alfred Adler: Theory and application. Retrieved from http://alfredadler.edu/about/alfred-adler-theory -application

Daniels, V. (2003). Erich Fromm. Retrieved from https://www.sonoma .edu/users/d/daniels/frommnotes.html

Horney, K. (1950). *Neurosis and human growth: The struggle toward self-realization.* New York, NY: W.W. Norton and Company, Inc.

Jung, C. G. (1947). *On the nature of the psyche.* London: Ark Paperbacks.

Kelly, G. A. (1963). *A theory of personality: The psychology of personal constructs.* New York, NY: Norton.

May, R. (2009). Rollo May on existential therapy. *Journal of Humanistic Psychology, 49*(4), 419–434.

McLeod, S. A. (2013). Erik Erikson. Retrieved from http://simply psychology.org/Erik-Erikson.html

McLeod, S. A. (2013). Sigmund Freud. Retrieved from http://www .simplypsychology.org/Sigmund-Freud.html

McLeod, S. A. (2014). Carl Rogers. Retrieved from http://www .simplypsychology.org.carl-rogers.html

McLeod, S. A. (2016). Abraham Maslow. Retrieved from http://www
.simlypsychology.org/maslow.html

McLeod, S. A. (2016). Albert Bandura. Retrieved from http://www
.simplypsychology.org/bandura.html

McLeod, S. A. (2016). Behaviorist Approach. Retrieved from http://www
.simplypsychology.org/behaviorism.html

Mischel, W. (2004). Toward and integrative science of the person. *Annual Review of Psychology, 55*, 1–22.

Rotter, J. (1982). *The development and applications of social learning theory.* New York, NY: Praeger.

CHAPTER 5

AGE—The European Older People's Platform. (2004). Age barriers: Older people's experience of discrimination in access to goods, facilities and services. Retrieved from http://www.age-platform.eu/images/stories/AGE_doc_goods_and_services_2_Dec_2004.pdf

Brown, M., Pitt-Catsouphes, M., McNamara, T. K., & Besen, E. (2014). Returning to the workforce after retiring: A job demands, job controls, social support perspective on job satisfaction. *The International Journal of Human Resource Management, 25*(22), 3113–3133.

Chung, J., Park, J., Cho, M., Park, Y., Kim, D., Yang, D., & Yang, Y. (2015). A study on the relationships between age, work experience, cognition, and work ability in older employees working in heavy industry. *Journal of Physical Therapy Science, 27*(1), 155–157.

Hansen, J. C., & Leuty, M. E. (2012). Work values across generations. *Journal of Career Assessment, 20*(1), 34–52.

Ruggs, E. N., Hebl, M. R., Walker, S. S., & Fa-Kaji, N. (2014). Selection bases that emerge when age meets gender. *Journal of Managerial Psychology, 29*(8), 1028–1043.

Twenge, J. M. (2016). Do millennials have a lesser work ethic? *Psychology Today*. Retrieved from https://www.psychologytoday.com/blog/our-changing-culture/201602/do-millennials-have-lesser-work-ethic

Twenge, J. M., Campbell, S. M., Hoffman, B. J., & Lance, C. E. (2010). Generational differences in work values: Leisure and extrinsic values increasing, social and intrinsic values decreasing. *Journal of Management, 36*(5), 1117–1142.

U.S. Equal Employment Opportunity Commission. Age discrimination. Retrieved from https://www.eeoc.gov/laws/types/age.cfm

CHAPTER 6

Bücker, J. J. L. E., Furrer, O., Poutsma, E., & Buyens, D. (2014). The impact of cultural intelligence on communication effectiveness, job satisfaction, and anxiety for Chinese host country managers working for foreign multinationals. *The International Journal of Human Resource Management, 25*(14), 2068–2087.

Evans, J. M., Lippoldt, D., & Marianna, P. (2001). Trends in working hours in OECD countries. Retrieved from https://www.ituc-csi.org/IMG/pdf/survey_ra_2016_eng.pdf

Freese, M., & Zapf, D. (1994). Action as the core of work psychology: A German approach. In H. C. Triandis, M. D. Dunnette, & L. M. Hough (Eds.), (1994). *Handbook of industrial and organizational psychology* (2nd ed., vol. 4). Palo Alto, CA: Consulting Psychologists Press.

Hofstede, G. (1984). *Culture's consequences: International differences in work-related values* (2nd ed.). Beverly Hills, CA: SAGE Publications.

International Trade Union Confederation. (2016). New ITUC global rights index—The world's worst countries for workers. Retrieved from https://www.ituc-csi.org/IMG/pdf/survey_ra_2016_eng.pdf

Kanai, A. (2008). Karoshi (work to death) in Japan. *Journal of Business Ethics, 84,* 209–216.

Lane, H.W., & Maznevski, M.L. (2014). *International Management Behavior: Global and Sustainable Leadership.* New York: John Wiley and Sons.

Miller, G. E. (2017). The U.S. is the most overworked developed nation in the world—when do we draw the line? Retrieved from https://20somethingfinance.com/american-hours-worked-productivity-vacation/

Nisen, M. (2013). The 10 countries with the world's best workers. *Business Insider.* Retrieved from http://www.businessinsider.com/countries-with-the-best-workers-2013-10

Shah, R. (2014). "The culture map" shows us the differences in how we work worldwide. Retrieved from http://www.forbes.com/sites/rawnshah/2014/10/06/the-culture-map-shows-us-how-we-work-worldwide/#6e6ed12a6e4f

About the Author and Contributors

Rudy Nydegger, PhD, ABPP, is professor emeritus of psychology and management at Union College and Union Graduate College in Schenectady, New York. He is coauthor of *Understanding Workplace Violence* and author of *Understanding and Treating Depression*, *Dealing with Anxiety*, and *Suicide and Mental Health*. He has written numerous chapters in other books and sections of encyclopedias. He has also published many articles and research studies. He is Board Certified in Clinical Psychology and a Distinguished Fellow in the National Academies of Practice.

Colby Enides, MA, MSW, received a bachelor's degree in criminal justice from SUNY Delhi and a dual master's degree in criminal justice and social work from SUNY Albany. She interned with the YWCA and the Schenectady County DA's office as a domestic violence advocate and then with the Independent Living Center of New York as a transition specialist, helping people transition back into their communities from nursing homes. She also interned with the Albany ACT (Assertive Community Treatment) team as a clinical social worker, assisting clients who had severe and persistent mental illnesses. She is presently working as an individual counselor with Hospitality House in Albany, New York, a long-term treatment center for adult males who have a drug addiction. Her research interests include organizational functioning and health policy.

Liesl A. Nydegger, PhD, MPH, earned her PhD in health promotion sciences with a concentration in global health and her master's in public health in health promotion, education, and evaluation from Claremont Graduate University, School of Community and Global Health. Currently, Dr. Nydegger is an assistant professor in the Department Kinesiology & Health Education at the University of Texas at Austin. Dr. Nydegger was awarded a Fulbright-Fogarty Fellowship in 2012–2013 that took place in South Africa. In 2015, Dr. Nydegger was awarded a two-year Ruth L. Kirschstein Institutional National Research Service Award Postdoctoral Research Fellowship at the Center for AIDS Intervention Research at the Medical College of Wisconsin. Dr. Nydegger's research interests include HIV prevention among survivors of violence, people who use drugs, and international populations.

Robert S. Rycroft, PhD, professor of economics, earned an MA (1974) and PhD (1978) from the University of Maryland, after receiving a BA (1972) in economics from the College of William and Mary. He has been a member of the faculty at the University of Mary Washington since 1977. A member of Phi Beta Kappa and the American Economic Association, Dr. Rycroft is the author of *Essentials of Macroeconomics I and II* (1989), *Hits on the Web: Mankiw Edition* (2003, with Carol Lee Clark and Michael R. Dowd), and *The Economics of Inequality, Discrimination, Poverty, and Mobility* (2009, 2nd edition 2017); the editor of *The Economics of Inequality, Poverty and Discrimination in the 21st Century* (2013) and *The American Middle Class: An Economic Encyclopedia of Progress and Poverty* (2017); and a contributor to *The Economics Problem Solver* and *GRE Economics Test.* He has published articles in the *International Journal of Forecasting*, the *Journal of Economic Education, Computers in Higher Education Economics Review*, and the *Nebraska Journal of Economics and Business.*

Amber L. Stephenson, PhD, MPH, is an assistant professor at the Clarkson University School of Business. Her research concerns organizational identification or the propensity of an individual to define the self in terms of an entity, specifically as it relates to satisfaction, turnover intention, performance outcomes, and retention. Her manuscripts have been featured in journals such as *Health Care Management Review, Health Promotion Practice, Services Marketing Quarterly, International Journal of Nonprofit and Voluntary Sector Marketing, International Review on Public and Nonprofit Marketing, International Journal of Education Management, Higher Education, Journal of College Student Retention*, and *Journal of Policy*

Research in Tourism, Leisure and Events. Prior to joining Clarkson University, Dr. Stephenson was the director and senior research associate at Temple University's Nonprofit Evaluation Services and Training (NEST) program where she managed research, evaluation, programming, and capacity-building exercises for partner organizations and state agencies.

Index